To

A tyrant book

P.S. evil king
Charles is one
of them !!

CW01475812

A SHORT HISTORY *of the* WORLD *in* 50 TYRANTS

Also in the series:

A SHORT HISTORY

 *of the*

WORLD *in*

50 TYRANTS

Ben Gazur

Illustrated by Peter Liddiard

Michael O'Mara Books Limited

First published in Great Britain in 2025 by
Michael O'Mara Books Limited
9 Lion Yard
Tremadoc Road
London SW4 7NQ

EU representative:
Authorised Rep Compliance Ltd
Ground Floor
71 Baggot Street Lower
Dublin D02 P593
Ireland

A CIP catalogue record for this book is available from the British
Library.

This product is made of material from well-managed, FSC®-certified
forests and other controlled sources. The manufacturing processes
conform to the environmental regulations of the country of origin.

For further information see
www.mombooks.com/about/sustainability-climate-focus
Report any safety issues to product.safety@mombooks.com and see
www.mombooks.com/contact/product-safety

UK editions:
ISBN: 978-1-78929-843-7 in hardback print format
ISBN: 978-1-78929-844-4 in trade paperback print format
ISBN: 978-1-78929-845-1 in ebook format

US editions:
ISBN: 978-1-78929-895-6 in hardback print format
ISBN: 978-1-78929-937-3 in ebook format

1 2 3 4 5 6 7 8 9 10

Jacket design and illustrations by Patrick Knowles
Typeset by Barbara Ward
Interior illustrations by Peter Liddiard
Printed and bound by CPI Group (UK) Ltd, Croydon, CR0 4YY

www.mombooks.com

MIX
Paper | Supporting
responsible forestry
FSC
FSC® C013604

For my beloved husband Michael,
the tyrant of my heart.

CONTENTS

Part III: Early Modern History

Part IV: Modern History

INTRODUCTION

ON THE NATURE OF TYRANNY

Human beings can have the unfortunate habit of choosing to do things which are diametrically opposed to their own best interests. Philosophers, scientists and theologians have taught for thousands of years that a simple life and simple pleasures are the best paths to happiness. Yet when people are offered the choice between a life of quiet contentment and a life of power over their fellow humans, they will often pick the latter. Human nature is complicated.

Tyrants are the culmination of the human desire to dominate others. There is no single definition of tyranny, but we know it when we see it. In the classical world, a tyrant was a man (it was always a man) who came to power through unconstitutional means. One of the most famous plays from antiquity, usually called today by its Latin name *Oedipus Rex*

– 'Oedipus the King' – was known to the Greeks as *Oidipous Tyrannos* – 'Oedipus the Tyrant' – because Oedipus had no claim to his throne: he took it by marrying the widow of the former king.

Over time, the definition of tyrant has grown to encompass any leader who has taken near absolute power into their own hands. When the tyrant speaks, it becomes the law. Tyranny is usually accompanied by repressive laws, harsh punishments and cruel oppressions. Some of those who have been called tyrants came to power by legitimate means but, unaccountably, seem to never give up their position. At least until someone decides they could do a better job and the tyrant's career is ended by the barrel of a gun or a hangman's noose. Everyone seems to think they should be the tyrant and so everyone is a threat in the tyrant's mind.

The Roman politician and writer Cicero (who contended with tyrants in his own time) told a curious tale about Dionysius I, the tyrant of Syracuse. For all his wealth and power, Dionysius had to fear for his life every day – he refused to let a barber shave him because he could not trust any of them not to slit his throat with a razor. Even his own wives had to be searched for weapons before he bedded them. Despite shutting himself up inside a prison of his own making there were still those who envied Dionysius and his position.

When Damocles, one of his courtiers, complimented Dionysius on his luck, the tyrant carried out a little experiment.

For a single evening he placed Damocles in the ruler's place at the head of the table during a feast. All manner of dainty foods were served up to Damocles on golden plates. Perfumes were daubed on him by attractive women and his wine was prepared by handsome youths. Damocles should have been the happiest man on Earth – but Dionysius had suspended a sword by a single horsehair above Damocles' head. At any moment it might have fallen and killed Damocles, and suddenly none of the kingly pleasures on offer seemed all that enjoyable anymore.

Although the moral of the story about the Sword of Damocles is an obvious one, we will see that history shows many people have not learned it. However, perhaps we should remember that early historians often nursed grudges, biases and hatreds. In particular, some writers were provoked by religious differences or a patriarchal dislike of strong female rulers to condemn their leaders as cruel despots. So, while some of the usurpers in this book probably did not behave any worse than their predecessors or successors, they have gone down in history as monsters.

The entire history of the world can be told just from the story of the tyrants who have ruled over it. This is either a deeply depressing record that reveals the truly abject state of human affairs – or it may be a more hopeful one when we look at the unpleasant ends which many tyrants meet. It may be cold comfort indeed to their victims, but we will see that no tyranny lasts forever. If there is a tendency to tyranny in mankind then there is also an unquenchable thirst for freedom. Let's hope freedom wins in the end.

I

ANCIENT HISTORY

· · ✖ · ·

GYGES OF LYDIA

. . . .

To the ancient Greeks, the definition of a tyrant was a person who took power illegitimately or by unusual means. Few tyrants are said to have had a more unorthodox path to the throne than King Gyges of the ancient kingdom of Lydia, in modern Turkey. Many strange tales are told about how he became king around 680 BCE – but all agree that Gyges had no right to the crown.

According to *The Histories* of Herodotus, the key to Gyges' usurpation was seduction. Gyges was captain of the guards of King Candaules, who, apparently unusually for the time, seemed to have fallen in love with his own queen. He was so enraptured by her beauty that he simply had to parade her in all her naked glory in front of his captain. Candaules planned to have Gyges hide within her bedroom so he could observe the queen without her ever knowing about the peeping Tom. The plan went awry, with disastrous results for Candaules.

After the queen had undressed that night she spotted Gyges slipping out of the room and immediately knew what had happened. Instead of confronting Candaules, she kept her rage at this treatment quiet but plotted revenge for her shame. Having secured the loyalty of the household, she summoned Gyges and told him there were only two options: either Candaules should be killed for planning to present her nakedness to his men, or Gyges would die for actually seeing her naked. Perhaps unsurprisingly, Gyges chose to kill Candaules and marry the queen himself to steal the throne. Candaules was slain in the night as he slept, one of the first palace coups in recorded history.

As Herodotus is known as both the Father of History and the Father of Lies, we should treat his version of events in the rise of Gyges with a little suspicion. Other sources also suggest that Gyges had no legitimate claim to his kingdom – but all confirm that he managed to hold onto his ill-gotten crown, at least for a time.

The truth of the rise of Gyges was probably more prosaic than the legends suggest. Around this time a group of nomadic horse-lords known as the Cimmerians had started to invade the region. Several Greek cities had been destroyed by the Cimmerians and it is likely that Candaules had failed to adequately protect his kingdom from the invaders. The Cimmerians may even have destroyed his capital. Losing a war is not good for the health

THE RING OF GYGES

The philosopher Plato told a myth about Gyges and his rise to power. In this tale, Gyges, or one of his ancestors, found a magic ring which granted him invisibility. Unseen, he entered the palace and seduced the queen. With her help, Gyges murdered his way to the throne without anyone seeing the crimes he committed.

when you are a king. Gyges may have used his position as captain of the guard to rid himself of the weak Candaules while offering stronger leadership to the Lydians.

How do you convince people that you should be the king after you have killed the old one? Religion, as we will see again and again, is a powerful tool in the hands of the powerful. When the people grew restive after Gyges stole the crown, Herodotus tells us he turned to the oracles of Greece and other places to seek the blessings of the gods for his actions. When the priests at Delphi said that Gyges was ordained to rule Lydia, the people duly accepted him as divinely appointed. Perhaps the massive amounts of gold and silver Gyges sent to Delphi had some effect on the will of the gods, as interpreted by the priests, who liked such gifts.

Gyges' wealth soon became proverbial. The ancient poet Archilochus, who lived around the same time, declared that he did not care for all the riches of Gyges – he preferred to avoid the dangers of lofty despotism. Tyrants may enjoy the treasures and luxuries which come with power but they must weigh that against the danger of their position.

There were many powerful kingdoms in the region and complex diplomatic relationships existed throughout the Near East. The Neo-Assyrian empire was one of the most formidable states at the time and so an upstart kingdom like Lydia, already beset by invasions, had to placate them. We know from Assyrian records that Gyges sent several embassies and rich gifts to the rulers of the empire to win their favour. He also formed alliances with several of the small Greek city-states which occupied the coastline of modern Turkey.

Gyges, who had come to power as military strongman, also felt the need to bolster his position by launching attacks against some of his neighbours. These were usually weak states, but even so Gyges did not always manage to conquer the lands he attacked, and those he did were often able to soon throw off his rule. Luckily for Gyges, he did seize an area with rich gold mines and successfully integrated it into his kingdom.

As long as a tyrant is able to offer money and gifts to their supporters, they can buy a certain amount of loyalty, and it seems as if Gyges never ran out of wealth. When Gyges fell, it came through hubris. Feeling secure in his kingdom, Gyges answered a call from King Psamtik I of Egypt to send an army to help him fight off rivals. Psamtik was successfully secured on his throne and Gyges won a powerful ally. However, his choice of friendship also earned him dangerous enemies in the form of Egypt's neighbours.

Egypt and the Neo-Assyrian Empire had been the major powers of the region, but now it seemed as if Gyges was projecting his influence well beyond his own borders. In Assyria this move was met with disapproval. It is always dangerous to send an army abroad when it might be needed at home – and Gyges soon found himself in desperate need of a defensive force.

The Cimmerians, who had been instrumental in creating the conditions for Gyges to become king, attacked Lydia yet again. The Assyrians had found it useful to allow the Cimmerians to continue some of their activities in Lydia as they helped to control the power of the Greek states. Gyges, while remaining friendly with the Assyrians and offering gifts, had always refused to send formal tribute to their kings. For the grand rulers of an empire, this seemed an unreasonably haughty position for a jumped-up usurper. When the Cimmerians attacked Lydia this time, there was no hope of any aid from Assyria.

The Cimmerians struck deeply into Lydia, and had allied to those local states who looked on the rise of a belligerent Lydia as a danger to their own security. The Cimmerians laid siege to Sardis, capital of Lydia, and managed to ravage the city. At some point in the war, around 652 BCE, Gyges died, probably slain in battle.

had come to power by violence during a time of
nd he left power under the same conditions. As we
it is ever thus with tyrants.

PHALARIS OF AKRAGAS

The gods occasionally punish even those most devoted to them. In the year 570 BCE the people of the city of Akragas, modern-day Agrigento in Sicily, decided to build a new temple to Zeus in their citadel as an act of piety. When a certain Phalaris offered to undertake the construction at a fixed price and within a fixed time period, the city gave him full access to the citadel, the fortified centre of the city. This proved to be a mistake. Once Phalaris was given the money, he used it to hire a group of mercenaries and led them into the citadel.

Soon afterwards he announced that many of the building materials had been stolen – a sacrilegious act which scandalized the people. He was then given powers to investigate the theft and bring those responsible to justice. He was also allowed to increase the defences around the temple site to stop further robberies. Phalaris created an impregnable fortress. Then, while the people were attending a religious festival, Phalaris led his mercenaries out, released all the slaves in the city to bolster his numbers, and killed any man who might threaten his position. By these clever and deceitful means, Phalaris was able to become tyrant of Akragas.

The last thing a new tyrant needs is a well-armed citizenry who might rise up and oppose them. Once Phalaris was in power, he ordered magnificent games to be held outside the city's wall and invited the populace to attend. As soon as they were outside, the gates of the city were slammed shut and locked. No one was allowed back in until every house had been searched and all weapons removed.

That, at least, is the story of Phalaris' rise to power that has come down to us. It is hard to untangle the truth from the myths about Phalaris as, within a short time, his name became a byword for the worst excesses of a tyrant's cruelty. Some insisted that Phalaris had a taste for feasting on suckling babies. It was reported that he boiled his enemies alive in gigantic cauldrons, or pitched them head first into pits filled with fire. But there was one invention which brought Phalaris immortal fame and immortal damnation – the Brazen Bull.

Morality is often flexible when one is offered sufficient amounts of money. Once word got out that Phalaris had a taste for torture, clever people from across the Greek world flocked to his court to offer up new methods for inflicting pain. One of the inventors who came to Akragas was Perilaus of Athens, who claimed to have a musical solution to Phalaris' enemies.

Perilaus constructed a bronze statue of a bull which was hollow and had a small hatch on the side into which a person

could be crammed. Once the victim was trapped a fire would be kindled under the belly of the beast to roast the prisoner to death. Since screams could be produced by any form of torture, Perilaus inserted a series of tubes into the mouth of the bull which would turn the shrieks of pain into a melodious bellowing. Perilaus expected a great honour, but those who serve tyrants should be ready for treachery.

The first victim of the Brazen Bull was Perilaus himself, who was unceremoniously shoved inside and slowly baked. The bull worked exactly as expected and Perilaus' only reward was to be taken out before completely dead and killed by some less painful method. The Brazen Bull might seem like a simple fable, but many early sources agree about its existence. The poet Pindar, who wrote about fifty years after Phalaris died, described the Brazen Bull in all its gory glory, and the bull itself was later seized by the Romans as war booty.

A tyrant who offers nothing but torture to his people can only survive for so long before he is overthrown. However, Phalaris was something of a military genius and used the same wiles he had employed to come to power in wars against the enemies of Akragas.

When Phalaris led his forces against the neighbouring Sicanian people, he was unable to break into their city. He learned that they had sufficient grain stored to withstand a lengthy siege, so it seemed that the war was hopeless. Instead of giving up, Phalaris entered into peace negotiations which allowed him to mingle with the Sicanians. He used this opportunity to bribe those in charge of the food stores, paying them to remove parts of the roof above the grain. When it rained, the grain rotted and the Sicanians were forced by hunger to surrender.

On another occasion, during his wars against the city of Vessa, he proposed a marriage between himself and the daughter of one of their rulers. He is said to have ordered some of his soldiers to shave their beards and dress as women. They then carried gifts into the city as part of the negotiations – and once inside slew all the defenders and handed the city to Phalaris.

The victories of tyrants tend to prolong their lives by making them seem to be a useful and necessary evil to their subjects. But even the most impressive general can outstay their welcome if they oppress their people too brutally. It is not known why the citizens of Akragas turned against Phalaris but when they did, they were led by a man called Telemachus. In around 544 BCE, Phalaris was captured by the rebels. He is said to have met a poetically satisfying fate – Phalaris was the last victim of his own Brazen Bull.

INHERITANCE OF FREEDOM

Theron of Akragas, despite being a descendent of the Telemachus who overthrew Phalaris, is said to have become a tyrant himself. In a manner very similar to Phalaris' own rise, he used public money to hire an army to conquer Akragas.

When tyrants fall, they seldom fall alone. After Phalaris was put down, it is said that the people of Akragas burned to death all of his friends, and his mother for good measure. They also passed a law banning anyone from wearing the colour blue because the tyrant made his retainers wear that colour.

Phalaris became something of a bogeyman in the ancient world; for centuries afterwards whenever a writer wanted to summon up an example of wicked tyranny they used Phalaris. The Roman author Cicero, fighting against the tyrants he saw rising around him, referred again and again to Phalaris as an example of the wretchedness of tyranny. Even as late as the fifth century CE, authors like Sidonius Apollinaris would refer to Phalaris' bloodlust, and Christian bishops described how their martyrs were suffering fates which even Phalaris in all his cruelty could not have imagined.

Not everyone has taken Phalaris as an exemplar of pure evil. Some writers suggested that he himself was not wicked, and only put Perilaus into the Brazen Bull as a fitting punishment for a corrupted genius. A strange and spurious text appeared in the Renaissance which claimed to be a collection of letters written by Phalaris in which he offered up opinions on the best way to rule a people. However, it would be a brave ruler who follows the example of Phalaris, unless they wish to end up being roasted alive.

POLYCRATES OF SAMOS

The island of Samos was a Greek state that was flourishing in the sixth century BCE, but also, it seems, there was some level of disorder. A vast temple of the goddess Hera was constructed around 560 BCE which would have been one of the wonders of the world. But in an unfortunate metaphor for the stability of the state, it was dismantled only ten years later when the ground beneath it began to sink.

Samos had belonged to the empire of the proverbially rich King Croesus of Lydia until his defeat by Persian forces in 547 BCE. The hold of the new Persian overlords on the island was tenuous and Samos offered a tempting target for any would-be tyrant looking for an opportunity to seize power. Polycrates of Samos was not about to let this chance slip his grasp.

According to later sources, Polycrates took advantage of a moment when the most powerful individuals in the state were at their most vulnerable. To thank the gods for their support, the citizens of Samos marched out of their city in full armour and regalia to visit a temple. At a key moment in the ritual, the men took off their armour to offer up prayers: that's when just seventeen of Polycrates' associates – including his two brothers, Pantagnotus and Syloson – struck.

While his brothers were murdering those who might oppose him, Polycrates had captured the citadel of the city and prepared to defend it. Apparently there was no need, and with just a little bloodshed he found himself in possession of a kingdom of his own. It helped that a tyrant from a neighbouring island also sent a military force to bolster Polycrates' coup. Tyrants tend to like dealing with other tyrants – they understand each other.

For a tyrant, the most dangerous thing you can do is trust anyone, even your own family. Though they had been instrumental in raising Polycrates to power, his brothers were soon removed as potential rivals. Pantagnotus was executed and Syloson was forced into exile, fleeing to the Persian court.

If a tyrant cannot find people to trust, he can at least always find useful friends willing to share in the success of their leader. Polycrates used these lieutenants to expand the domain of his rule.

Polycrates is credited with being the first of the Greek leaders to place the majority of his power in a strong navy. The islands of Greece and the coasts of Turkey could only be controlled by a formidable fleet and Polycrates invested much of his wealth in building 100 new warships. With these he created a thalassocracy, a sea empire. While the Persians were almost invincible on land, they had no real skill with seamanship, so a navy was all the protection against them that Samos and its tyrant needed. These vessels also functioned to create a trade network which brought goods, slaves and wealth into Samos.

Soon Polycrates' navy was launching attacks against neighbouring islands and smashing their defences. During one of his most notable victories, he captured a huge number of slaves and set them to work constructing the fortifications of Samos. His enemies built the very walls which would keep Polycrates safe if his navy ever failed.

Polycrates also set about beautifying his city with new constructions funded by his conquests. The ruined Temple of Hera was replaced with one even larger and more richly decorated (and built on steadier ground). The prosperity of Samos attracted thinkers, poets and engineers from across the

Greek world. The capital city grew until it could no longer be supplied with sufficient fresh water and so an aqueduct was created by digging a tunnel over a kilometre long to provide it with sweet water.

Samos waxed ever more powerful during this period and caught the attention of the other great powers of the Mediterranean. Polycrates' ships became notorious for plundering wherever they went, even striking against his allies. This did not concern Polycrates, as he said that when he stole from his enemies he kept what he took and when he stole from friends he received their gratitude by returning their goods to them and so made them more loyal.

The overwhelming successes enjoyed by Polycrates offered the Greek historian Herodotus the chance to contemplate the nature of fortune and the fates of tyrants. It may have more of fable and folktale than history to it, but Herodotus' tale of Polycrates and his ring became one of the most famous events associated with Samos.

Polycrates had formed an alliance with the Egyptian pharaoh Amasis II and was providing him with naval support as well as selling vast numbers of slaves to Egypt for use in their army. It was a highly profitable enterprise for both parties and so might have been a long-lasting partnership. But Amasis grew uneasy about how well Polycrates was doing. Surely the gods would not allow one man to have so many triumphs and such good fortune without striking him down to punish his hubris?

Amasis wrote to Polycrates and told him to take the thing he most valued in all the world and throw it away so that he might taste a little loss and so ward off the fury of the gods. Polycrates decided to follow this advice. He was a great collector of gemstones and had an especially valuable ring set with gorgeous jewels. Polycrates rowed out into the middle of the sea, took the ring from his finger, and cast it into the waves so as to lose it forever.

A few days later some fishermen presented themselves at the palace with a magnificent fish they had caught and offered it as a gift to Polycrates. Tyrants love free things and so it was accepted. While preparing it to eat, the fish was cut open and out tumbled Polycrates' lost ring. When Polycrates was handed this he wrote to Amasis and told him that fortune had restored his loss to him.

Rather than being impressed by this further mark of the gods' favour, Amasis immediately cut off his dealings with Polycrates. He knew that the gods would not suffer an endless stream of human good fortune and when Polycrates was eventually pulled down, Amasis did not want to fall with him. That, at least, is Herodotus' telling.

It does seem true that at some point Polycrates changed sides by allying with Persia against Egypt. He sent some of his warships, crewed by his least trustworthy citizens, to Persia with a note that the crews could be dispensed with and Persia could use the ships. When the fleet was out at sea, perhaps sensing treachery, the sailors rebelled against Polycrates and sailed to Greece. There they allied with Sparta and carried a Spartan army to Samos to drive out Polycrates. Their siege was unsuccessful partly due to Polycrates' defensive fortifications, but time was running out for the tyrant.

FIRST FORGERIES

Polycrates paid off the besiegers with some of the vast wealth he had accumulated. But even here he was wily. Herodotus tells us he used gold coins that were made with lead cores and just a thin layer of gold on the outside to pay his enemies. Examples of these false coins thought to date from Polycrates' forgery still exist.

By this point, without the financial might of Egypt backing him, Polycrates might finally have been running out of money. Accounts differ over what happened to cause his eventual defeat. Polycrates might have captured a Persian embassy sent to him, killed them and stolen their riches. Or the Persians simply wanted to finally bring Samos into their empire.

A Persian governor called Oroetes invited Polycrates to visit him, promising money that the Greek desperately needed. When Polycrates turned up, he was seized and crucified. The mightiest tyrant of the Greek world was hung out to rot in the open air. Later, Syloson, brother of the murdered ruler, was placed in power on Samos in the service of Persia.

AMASIS II

. . . .

Those who wish to steal a throne through force of arms do well to win the loyalty of the army – and do even better if they have shown themselves to be a formidable general. Amasis, also known as Ahmose, had taken part in a wildly successful Egyptian campaign to crush the kingdom of Kush to the south of Egypt in 592 BCE. Amasis served under Pharaoh Psamtik II in this war and may have been honoured for his valour, even though he came from a relatively humble position.

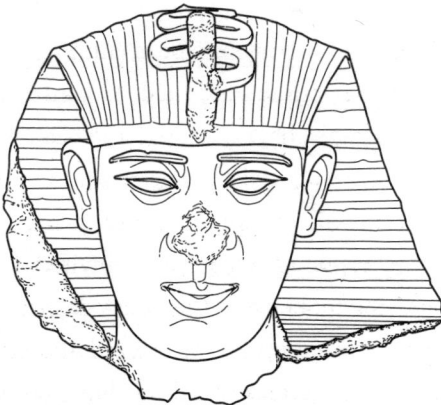

When Psamtik II died soon afterwards the throne passed to his son Apries. Apries aimed to restore Egypt to the glories of the distant past. He undertook grand building works and attempted to project his power into bordering lands. It is recorded that he tried to check the growth of Babylonian influence in the Near East by sending an army to protect the city of Jerusalem. This was a failure and the army retreated, allowing Jerusalem's fall and the Babylonian captivity of the Judeans.

Since Apries' father had been part of the great tradition of strong military pharaohs, the seeming weakness of their current pharaoh must have alarmed some Egyptians. There is evidence that at least one army camp at a strategic site rebelled against him, though this was rapidly suppressed. Apries turned to hiring Greek mercenaries to create a force that could stand against any threats from within and was loyal to him and his money alone.

There were military successes during Apries' reign which must have bolstered his authority. One attempted invasion of Egypt's borders by the Babylonians was repelled and Apries was able to bring a number of states under his control. When the King of Cyrene, which bordered Egypt to the west, faced a revolt of the Libyan population in 570 BCE, Apries saw an opportunity. The Libyans called for military assistance and so Apries sent a large force, but held his Greek mercenaries in reserve.

The campaign was a disaster. The Egyptians were soundly defeated and forced to retreat back towards Egypt. Grumbling began among the men that their loss could only be the result of treachery and that defeat had been Apries' aim from the start. If he could kill off the Egyptians in the army, then the only military force in the country would be the pharaoh's Greek army. They declared themselves in open rebellion.

What happened next is recorded by Herodotus, and must therefore be treated with a little suspicion, but Apries sent Amasis to quell the revolt. As soon as Amasis arrived in the camp, the men placed a crown on his head and declared him to be the new pharaoh. Whether Amasis had planned this usurpation all along is not recorded, but he took full advantage of the opportunity.

THE FART

When Apries learned that Amasis had claimed the throne, he sent emissaries to capture the rebel and bring him back. The officials presented their demand to Amasis. Amasis listened carefully, then lifted one leg and let out a resounding fart. 'Take that back to Apries as my reply,' he said.

When Apries sent demands that Amasis surrender and present himself before the real pharaoh, he was swiftly rebuffed. Amasis informed the messengers that he would indeed come and meet Apries, but he would be bringing his army with him.

Apries was utterly outmatched despite his Greek mercenaries, and seemed to have already lost the loyalty of his subjects. He was defeated, and Amasis was officially raised to the throne as Pharaoh Amasis II.

What happened next is unclear. Some sources say that Apries was killed immediately. Other records say that Apries fled to the Babylonians and raised a force there which invaded Egypt to win Apries his throne back. When this army was defeated, too, Apries was either killed in the fighting, or captured and held in splendid seclusion by Amasis II. Herodotus says that the Egyptian people resented their former pharaoh being treated well in his retirement, and so Amasis handed him over to them so they could execute him. It is rarely a good idea for a tyrant to keep a potential rival around, so Amasis was probably glad to be rid of Apries, however it happened.

Amasis set about securing his new reign. He may have married one of Apries' daughters to link himself to the former royal house and wash away some of the taint of his lowly birth. He rewarded his followers with honours, positions at court and wealth – the usual gifts handed out by tyrants. Some of his supporters did very well under the new order. Ahmose-sa-Neith was named as head of Amasis' guard, supervisor of works and head of the royal fleet. The monumental sarcophagus of Ahmose-sa-Neith still exists, as well as inscriptions set up hundreds of years later which show he was still revered long after his death.

Key to Amasis II's success was the fact that he returned prosperity to Egypt and made it richer than it had been for generations. He achieved this by integrating his realm into the economy of the wider Mediterranean and especially the Greek states. We have seen how he had dealings with Polycrates of Samos (see page 23). Like many tyrants, Amasis took on some of the characteristics of the regime which he had replaced. Through contact with the Greeks, he was able to recruit mercenaries to serve in his army, as well as bring in slaves.

The reign of Amasis II was a highlight of ancient Egyptian fortunes but the seeds of Egypt's downfall were sown by the pharaoh himself. Amasis quarrelled with one of his Greek mercenaries, who promptly fled to the Persian court and offered up all he knew about Egyptian defences. When Cambyses II of Persia requested an Egyptian princess as a wife, Amasis refused to send one of his own daughters so he sent a daughter of Apries. Sending the daughter of an enemy you killed to one of your most powerful enemies is strategically questionable. Predictably, she convinced Cambyses to invade Egypt.

Amasis II experienced another piece of good luck in 526 BCE by dying. During decades in power he had rarely suffered any serious setback, and was able to pass on his throne to his son, Psamtik III. Unfortunately for his dynasty, however, it was soon after Amasis' death that the might of Persia poured across the borders.

At the Battle of Pelusium the Egyptians and Persians clashed. Later historians say that the Persians carried sacred animals like cats in front of their troops and so the Egyptians refused to attack in case they hurt the animals. More likely the Egyptians were simply routed. Psamtik III retreated and was besieged in Memphis, where he was captured. His rule had lasted around six months. Egypt was taken into the growing Persian Empire.

If Amasis II had hoped that he would enjoy peace and the divine immortality which all pharaohs were destined to have after death, he was disappointed. Cambyses ordered that his tomb be broken open and Amasis' corpse dragged out. The body underwent several rounds of abuse and desecration before being burned and the ashes scattered to the winds.

HIPPIAS AND HIPPARCHUS

Sometimes tyranny is as heritable as freckles or curly hair. It is said that there were signs that the family of Peisistratus would prove to be dangerous before their first member was even born. According to Herodotus, the omen came when a man called Hippocrates offered a sacrifice at the Olympic Games a few years before 600 BCE. When Hippocrates placed the sacrificial meat into a cauldron of water it boiled over before the fire underneath it could even be lit. A nearby soothsayer noticed this sign and told Hippocrates to divorce his wife immediately and, should she give birth to a son, to abandon the baby at once.

Needless to say, Hippocrates did not follow this advice and, when his son Peisistratus was born, he raised the boy to take a place among the Athenian elite. Peisistratus was not content to be one among many – he wanted to be the entire elite. After winning fame as a general, Peisistratus attached himself to the faction of Athenians who lived outside the city in the hills, but their support was not enough to give him complete power.

One day around 561 BCE, Peisistratus rode into the heart of the marketplace of Athens in a state of alarm. He was covered in blood and his horses were similarly besmirched. To the people around him he declared that he had been attacked by his political enemies. He begged the crowd to provide him with a bodyguard, and the Athenians complied. With this new force of men Peisistratus seized the Acropolis at the heart of Athens and then took complete control of the city.

Whether or not this is exactly how Peisistratus took power, we do know that his family remained (on and off) the leaders of Athens until the end of the sixth century BCE. Though Athens was shorn of its freedom, Peisistratus gave its citizens increased influence in Greece through consolidating nearby lands under Athenian control. When Peisistratus died in 528 BCE, his two sons, Hippias and Hipparchus, stepped into the role of tyrants.

The brothers seem to have faced little discontent about the continuation of the tyranny. Though they and their father had endured periods of exile which interrupted Peisistratus' rule, in general he was well regarded by the majority of Athenians. Peisistratus had instituted the theatrical festivals of the Dionysia, expanded the celebrations of the festival in honour of Athena, and erected grand new buildings to beautify their city. His populist policies, which reduced the influence of the aristocratic families, had won the favour of the masses.

Hippias is generally considered to be the more important of the two sons, but Hipparchus shared in the control of the state. The brothers continued their father's tolerant form of tyranny and ruled without considerable unrest against them. In 514 BCE, however, their joint leadership came to an end due to a matter of the heart.

Among the Athenian upper classes, there was a long tradition of pederasty whereby an older man would woo an adolescent boy with gifts and begin a sexual relationship with him. The older lover would then lead the younger into society and, it was thought, prepare him to take his role as a citizen in Athens. This custom was not universally praised in Athens – the plays of Aristophanes are full of scurrilous and frank jokes about those who play the passive role in homosexual acts. Nonetheless, it persisted.

One pair of lovers at this time were the older Aristogeiton and his young paramour, Harmodius. By all accounts, Harmodius was a glorious youth who was lusted after by many, and among his admirers was the tyrant Hipparchus. For all the power and wealth of his position, Hipparchus did not appeal to Harmodius; the boy refused his advances but did not fail to tell Aristogeiton about them. It is always risky to turn down a tyrant, even more so to humiliate them. When it became known that Hipparchus had failed to win the 'hand' of Harmodius, the tyrant decided to take his revenge.

Harmodius had a sister and Hipparchus issued her an invitation to take part in the procession of the festival of Athena. This was a high honour for a young lady. But when she turned up to participate she was publicly driven away in front of the crowds on the grounds that only virgins could perform her role. A woman's virginity was highly guarded in Athens and Hipparchus had essentially declared Harmodius' sister to be a harlot. After this provocation, Aristogeiton and Harmodius decided to slay the tyrants.

Together with a few others, the pair plotted to strike during a religious ritual which both Hipparchus and Hippias planned to attend. The conspirators intended to take concealed daggers, stab the tyrants to death and liberate the city from their rule. However, on the day, the plan quickly went wrong. As Harmodius and Aristogeiton waited for the pre-planned moment for the assassinations, they saw one of their fellow conspirators approach Hippias and exchange a few words. Fearing they had been betrayed, they launched their attack, running up to Hipparchus with the aim of killing the one who had done them the most harm.

Hipparchus was brought down by series of savage wounds and bled to death. In the ensuing confusion, Aristogeiton was at first able to escape the tyrant's guards before being captured, but Harmodius was slaughtered where he stood. Hippias had everyone present searched to see who had a dagger on them and was therefore part of the plot, and Aristogeiton was tortured to reveal the names of other conspirators. However, he managed to insult Hippias so badly that the tyrant personally killed him.

Understandably, the murder of his brother somewhat soured Hippias. Though he had previously ruled fairly and generously, he began to grow bitter and harsh in his treatment of the Athenians. Executions of any who crossed him became common and many people were banished, including the most influential families in the city. His cruelty meant that Hippias no longer enjoyed the support of the people and he had never been fully trusted by the aristocrats. Hippias turned to the Persians in hopes of support, but allying himself to a foreign power did not make him any more popular.

One of the families that had been driven from the city tricked the Spartans into attacking Athens. Hippias was forced to retreat to the Acropolis, where his father had once started his rise to power, and eventually had to yield. He was sent into exile and, despite various attempts to regain the tyranny, never managed it.

During the Athenian democracy, the lovers Harmodius and Aristogeiton were treated as heroes who had struck against tyrants. Vases were painted with their images and marble statues sculpted showing them with the daggers they had used to try to free Athens.

TOOTHLESS TYRANTS

In 490 BCE, the exiled Hippias attempted to regain Athens by encouraging the Persians to invade. When he landed with their armies on Athenian soil, Hippias, by then an old man, suffered a coughing fit so severe that he coughed a tooth straight out of his mouth. This was considered a bad omen for the coming Battle of Marathon, which the Athenians duly won. Hippias died as he retreated with his Persian allies.

CINCINNATUS

Dictatorship is, outside of dictators and their cronies, universally thought of as a terrible fate for a state. Yet for the Romans, a dictator was, when the moment called for it, just the person to set everything right. A tradition of good dictators would in the end prove to be the perfect cover for tyrannical dictators to arise in Rome.

The origins of the Roman state are clouded in myth and mystery. Even the ancient Romans questioned some of the legends which were taught about the origins of their city. Everyone knows how Romulus and Remus were suckled by a she-wolf before founding the city. The historian Livy suggested that the she-wolf was in fact a prostitute – the cheapest sort of prostitutes were known as she-wolves.

The second most important myth of the Romans was how they had overthrown the monarchy which ruled them in their earliest days and set up a republic in its place. According to tradition there were seven kings of Rome and the last of them was driven out in around 509 BCE. The last king, Tarquin the Proud, proved to be an incompetent military leader and worse father. When his son raped a noblewoman, the ire of the nobles was roused. Under the leadership of Lucius Junius Brutus, the king was exiled and a new form of government adopted.

Since having all power in the hands of a single person had proved to be so disastrous to Rome, it was decided that power should always be divided between multiple people. At the head of the Republic were set two consuls who were elected to serve for a single year at a time, each able to veto the declarations of the other. In this way no one person could control the state.

Lucius Quinctius Cincinnatus was born in the final years of Rome under the kings but came of age when the Republic was still in its infancy. The early years of the Republic were violent ones. Rome controlled a tiny area of land with many rival states nearby, several of them working for the return of the kings. Within the city, there were murderous confrontations between the lower class plebeians and the wealthy patricians who held most of the power. In 460 BCE, Cincinnatus became consul when another consul was slain during a battle against a band of malcontents who had captured one of the hills of Rome.

Cincinnatus proved to be no friend of the common people and, in an echo of the bad behaviour of the final royal family, his son is said to have been exiled from Rome after murdering a plebeian. This should have been the end of Cincinnatus as a figure in Roman history. Once his consulship was over, Cincinnatus retired from Rome and tended his four acres of farmland on his estate in quiet solitude.

When, in about 458 BCE, the Aequi tribe invaded the land of a people allied to Rome, the Roman Senate voted to send out an army against them. Almost immediately, there was another military crisis when a force of soldiers attacked the territory of Rome itself. One of the consuls and his army became surrounded by the enemy, sparking panic that the city itself would soon be vulnerable to its enemies. When the remaining consul proved to be ineffective in the crisis, it was voted that a dictator be appointed, and that Cincinnatus should take control.

The exact origins of the dictatorship are murky, but according to the Republican constitution, in times of emergency complete governance of Rome could be handed to one man. This dictator would rank above the consuls and all other magistrates with no one able to countermand their orders, except perhaps the tribunes who represented the plebeians. While consuls were attended by twelve bodyguards called lictors, the dictator was surrounded by twenty-four. When a dictator was appointed, it was to deal with a specific crisis in the state, and it was thought that by placing them above the petty politics of the Senate they would be better able to deal with the issue. The dictatorship of Cincinnatus would test whether placing one person in charge would harm the Republic or save it.

When envoys from the Senate reached Cincinnatus' farm they discovered him performing manual labour on his land – traditionally he was said to have been ploughing his fields. On being told that he was dictator, he washed the mud and dust from his face, dressed in a toga and went to take command in Rome.

Cincinnatus ordered that all men of military age arm themselves and that all civilian activity which did not support the war should be stopped. With his new force he set out to attack the Aequi army that was menacing the Romans. In the battle that followed, the Aequi were completely overwhelmed and their leaders led before Cincinnatus in bondage. Instead of slaughtering the enemy, Cincinnatus is said to have simply stripped them of their arms and forced them to march away. The head of the Aequi army was taken to Rome and displayed among the captured booty during Cincinnatus' triumphal procession.

CURLY HAIR

Romans of high status had multiple names and the third name, known as the *cognomen*, often referred to a peculiar feature. Cicero, for instance, derives from the word for 'chickpea' and probably came from an ancestor with a growth on his face. The name Cincinnatus means 'curly hair' – and the dictator was the first to have this name – suggesting he had particularly curly locks.

Having taken all the actions necessary to secure Rome from its enemies, Cincinnatus stepped down from the dictatorship after just sixteen days in charge. He reputedly left the city at once and returned to his farm where he once again set about ploughing his land.

Historians today doubt that much of the tale of Cincinnatus is factually true, but to the later Romans at the end of the Republic it was one of their most potent legends. In the first century BCE, the Republic was fracturing under the strain of army commanders and politicians seeking ever greater authority. The threat of civil war was looming. It was only natural that many people longed for the Golden Age which was thought to have existed in the good old days of the young Republic, when the most powerful men were entirely honourable.

The longing for a good dictator to set the state in order may have been natural, but retelling the story of Cincinnatus as something to be hoped for might have had the opposite effect. Thinking a strong man is coming to save you might have prepared the ground for such a person, more unscrupulous than Cincinnatus, to emerge. The fields of the Roman state would prove to be as fertile as Cincinnatus' farm when it came to raising autocrats.

THE THIRTY TYRANTS

Following their success in driving back a vast Persian invasion force in 478 BCE, Sparta and Athens were left as the greatest powers in the Greek world. Each accrued allies, and the democracy that was Athens even formed something of an empire through setting up a network of allegiance called the Delian League. Athens experienced a golden age as money poured into it. Many of the most exquisite pieces of classical Greek art date from this period, as does the Parthenon which stands above Athens.

The glories of Athens bred arrogance among its people. In 431 BCE, Sparta and Athens fell into war with each other. The Peloponnesian War, as the conflict is known, raged back and forth for decades. Sparta would invade the land of the

Athenians and ravage it each summer, while the Athenian navy carried on the war at sea. The people of Athens withdrew for protection behind the Long Walls which connected the city to its port at Piraeus.

Though safe from the Spartan armies, nothing could save the Athenians from disease. In the cramped conditions behind the Long Walls, a plague emerged and spread rapidly, claiming thousands of victims, including the Athenian leader Pericles. Leadership of the democracy changed hands as the course of the war waxed and waned until, in 404 BCE, Athens was besieged by Spartan forces. When the city was forced to surrender one of the terms was that the Long Walls which had protected Athens were pulled down, which was done to the sound of flute girls playing jaunty tunes.

The Spartans would not allow the Athenians to keep their democracy either, whose fickle will had prolonged the bitter war. They insisted that thirty men be chosen to shape the new laws which would govern the city. These men soon became known as the Thirty Tyrants. Among their number were men who had previously attempted a coup, failed and fled into exile. They now returned for another try at power.

The Thirty Tyrants seem to have found that ruling directly suited them better than creating a new constitution. They created a body of 3,000 citizens who they drew into the government – it is always useful to make sure that as many hands are drenched in blood as possible, and creating a wide support base helps spread the blame for tyranny. The tyrants and their associates were the only men allowed to bear arms and to have full rights. To enforce their judgments, the Thirty also hired hundreds of men with whips to act as their strongmen and terrify those who gave even the slightest sign of disobedience.

There were those who stood against the Tyrants. The Athenians had always prized the concept of *isonomia* – equality before the law – and were used to speaking up against policies they did not like. The lucky ones who opposed the Thirty managed to flee the city. The unfortunate ones were executed without trial.

Among those who remained in the city was the philosopher Socrates. He was used to questioning everyone and everything in his search for truth and wisdom, and saw no need to stop now. He might even have felt somewhat safe as one of his former students, Critias, soon rose to leadership of the Thirty. Unfortunately, Critias turned out to be the most extreme of the tyrants, always calling for more power and more deaths.

The Thirty ordered Socrates and four other men to arrest Leon of Salamis and bring him in for execution, so that the five would be tainted with association with the tyranny. Socrates refused to do anything unjust and so he simply went home without doing it, while the other four did what they were told. Historically, 80 per cent seems to be roughly the proportion of those who will obey the orders of a tyrant, even in the most wicked of crimes. Socrates escaped punishment for this, perhaps because he had educated so many of the new rulers, but the Thirty could no longer tolerate him going around the marketplace and educating people in how to think for themselves. The Thirty forbade Socrates to teach, perhaps fearing that it would lead to his students asking too many questions in the Socratic style about the nature of authority.

SOCRATIC WISDOM

During the rule of the Thirty Tyrants, Socrates came across an acquaintance in a furious rage. When Socrates asked why he was so upset, the man replied that the Thirty had refused to give him a position of power. Socrates replied. 'Are you annoyed then that you are not a tyrant too?'

As often happens when power is wielded by a small clique, even other members of the original revolutionary group become suspect. Theramenes, one of the moderate tyrants, was hauled up on trial by Critias as a danger to the tyrants. But it became clear that the jury was disposed to acquit Theramenes. To prevent this, Critias organized a group of armed men to surround the court and remove Theramenes from the list of the Thirty and their associates. He therefore lost his right to a trial at all. When presented with the hemlock at his execution soon afterwards, Theramenes drank it quickly, and then poured out a little toast of the poison 'To the health of my beloved Critias!'

Because the Athenians were addicted to literature, the actions of the Tyrants were recorded by a number of writers. A speech by the orator Lysias reveals how the Thirty operated and the horror that Athenians later felt about their actions: 'So enormous, so numerous are the acts they have committed, that neither could lying avail one to accuse them of things more monstrous than the actual facts, nor with every desire to speak mere truth could one tell the whole.'

Lysias' brother Polymarchus was a wealthy philosopher whom the Thirty targeted for death to steal his money. To pretend that this was not purely a cash grab, the tyrants arrested him along with nine others, two of whom were poor. Every article of wealth was taken from Polymarchus, even the gold earrings in his wife's ears were snatched away, and he was forced to drink deadly hemlock without ever being put on trial.

The tyrant Eratosthanes was later questioned by Lysias about his role in the arrest of Polymarchus. Eratosthenes fell back on a defence which would be used again and again by the servants of despots. 'I was just,' he said, 'following orders.'

When tyrants drive out their enemies, who may all have differing politics, they create a group who will be unified by their desire to destroy the tyrant. The exiles from Athens flocked to a general called Thrasybulus whom the Thirty had exiled. Soon a force was raised against the Thirty and it moved in to attack. The Thirty sent ambassadors to Sparta to ask that a garrison could be sent to Athens to shore up their control. Relying on the support of a foreign, and hated, power did not endear the tyrants to the Athenians.

With a thousand men, Thrasybulus captured the port of Piraeus and withstood an attack by a larger force sent by the Thirty. In the melee, Critias was killed. The surviving Thirty fled the city as the exiles battled their way towards Athens. The brutal rule of the Thirty Tyrants had lasted for just thirteen months. In the aftermath of their fall, the democracy was restored.

QIN SHI HUANG

In 1974, a family of farmers near Xi'an in China were digging a well to water their pomegranate groves when their spades struck something. When they examined the hole, they discovered that it contained the head of a life-size figure sculpted in terracotta. When archaeologists arrived to excavate the site they soon turned up more figures, and then hundreds more, all dating from the third century BCE. The farmers had stumbled upon the Terracotta Army – built to protect the tomb of Qin Shi Huang, first Emperor of China.

From the fifth to the third centuries BCE, China was divided between a number of states all vying to conquer the others. Understandably, historians call this time the Warring States Period. The Zhou dynasty, who had been the last kings of China, maintained their position as nominal kings while the almost totally independent states were ruled by dukes. As time went on these dukes threw off even this token subservience and began making themselves kings in name as well as reality.

The state of Qin in western China grew in power in the fourth century BCE. Following the twists and turns of Chinese kingdoms in this period would require the work of history books as long as the Great Wall. But suffice to say that by the time Zhao Zheng, the future first emperor, was born to the king of Qin in 259 BCE, the Qin were at war with most of the other states.

Zhao Zheng came to the throne when just thirteen years old and ruled under the regency of his powerful mother and her associates, a number rumoured to be her lovers. When one, Lao Ai, attempted to replace the young king, Zhao Zheng raised an army, drove the conspirators and their forces from the field, and had Lao Ai torn apart by horses. Now in full control of his kingdom, the young man turned his attention to his warring neighbours. He had no taste for just being one among many. All of China would be his.

You don't conquer the known world without making a few enemies, and some of them tried to strike back. There were a number of assassination attempts on the king of Qin. In one of them, a famed musician turned up to play at court, but it was soon realized he intended to kill Zhao Zheng. Zheng was not a philistine, so instead of killing the would-be assassin he simply had his eyes cut out and made him perform his intended concert. The assassin was not to be deterred however and when the king approached to congratulate him on his skill, the musician swung his stringed instrument (which had been turned into a bludgeon with concealed weights). Being blind he missed and was executed for his troubles.

The ruthlessness which preserved the king's life served him well in warfare. From 230 BCE, the armies of the Qin marched out against their rivals who fell one by one. The Qin used diplomatic wiles as well as brute force to bring all of China under their sway. They bribed states like the Qi not to come to the aid of the other states – and then turned on the Qi when they were the final state left free. The final king of Qi, Tian Jian, was captured in 221 BCE without much of a fight and bundled into an ignominious exile where he starved to death. Zhao Zheng was now king of all of China.

Except king was no longer a sufficient title for Zhao Zheng. After all there had been many kings, but all had now fallen to him. To exalt himself above them, he named himself Emperor of China, and is known to history as Qin Shi Huang (First Qin emperor). Having conquered his vast domains, Qin Shi Huang set about reorganizing them so that he could hold onto them. No longer would the lords be able to defy the rule of the great leader. To mark the new control of the state, all of the weapons of his enemies were taken, melted down and crafted into twelve gigantic statues each weighing around forty tons. This would be a monumental reign in all regards.

With his reordering of all matters in the country, it began to feel like a new beginning of history, so what better way to mark this new start than by destroying history? Qin Shi Huang ordered the burning of nearly all books on history and philosophy in the entire country. After all, people with access to that knowledge might use it to compare the current ruler unfavourably to the past. Possession of banned books was a capital crime, but to use history to criticize the emperor meant the death of your entire family. Only books with practical advice on farming, building and manufacturing, plus a few 'classics' such as Confucius' *Analects*, were spared. By burning the books of the various groups of philosophers known as the Hundred Schools of Thought, the emperor limited access to ways of thinking other than his own.

It is one thing to secure your empire from internal threats but another to keep enemies out. Qin Shi Huang ordered the construction of the first Great Wall of China, which connected previous defences into a single barrier against raiders from the north. This vast undertaking required all of the infrastructure of roads, canals and manpower which Qin Shi Huang had reorganized. Thousands died in the harsh conditions of the areas where the wall was built. It was a common punishment for criminals to be sentenced to work on the wall – almost a death sentence. Folk tales sprang up about its many horrors: blood was said to make up the mortar.

The one thing that no earthly leader can defend against is death; even the thickest wall cannot keep it out. Qin Shi Huang became obsessed with the finding an elixir of immortality which was mentioned in Chinese mythology, philosophy and alchemical teachings. Work on these elixirs involved the creation of many techniques which pushed forward the science of chemistry, but also pushed many into the grave as the alchemists worked with deadly materials like lead compounds and mercury.

When the alchemists failed to produce an elixir of immortality that pleased Qin Shi Huang, he is said to have

FATAL IMMORTALITY

Mercury is well known today to be highly toxic and repeated exposure can lead to a number of physical and mental problems. Its liquid metallic appearance made it seem almost magical, and so it was used in a number of elixirs of immortality created by Chinese alchemists for Chinese emperors. Ironically, the very things meant to preserve their lives may have killed many who took it.

ordered that 460 of them be buried alive as a public warning to others. The deterrent seems to have worked: one expedition sent out to foreign lands to look for the elixir simply disappeared. It is thought they feared to return empty-handed. All of the mercury which Qin Shi Huang ingested in his search for eternal life probably made him mentally unstable and could have brought about his death in 210 BCE, aged just forty-nine. He was placed in a massive tomb complex with his thousands of terracotta warriors and, it is thought, surrounded by lakes and rivers of the very mercury which might have killed him. Certainly, the ground around his tomb shows suspiciously high levels of mercury.

The Qin dynasty did not long outlive its founder. Qin Shi Huang's son, Qin Er Shi, ruled for just three years before being deposed and forced to commit suicide.

SULLA

. . . . .

In 82 BCE, the Roman general Lucius Cornelius Sulla called a meeting of the Senate. Outside of the Senate House 6,000 of his enemies, captured in battle, were lined up. As the senators waited with hushed breath to find out what Sulla intended to do with them, they suddenly heard the shrill screams of men being executed. All of the prisoners were being slaughtered. Sulla commanded the senators not to pay any attention to what was happening outside but just to listen to his words. It was clear that there was a new master in Rome.

The Roman Republic which had been so successful in conquering the Mediterranean world was at this juncture beginning to destroy itself. There had always been political fighting in Rome as the patricians jostled with the plebeians and politicians aligned themselves with either the rich minority or the masses. Street violence and murder were almost expected tactics in debates. But in the first century BCE, these struggles changed from nuisances to actual dangers to the Republic. The armies fielded by Rome grew larger and the resources military commanders could call on grew greater, but the sacrosanct law was that no general could ever enter Rome at the head of his legions. While that tradition was respected, the Senate could remain supreme.

Rome at this time controlled the entire Italian peninsula but not all Italians were Roman citizens. Most were allies of Rome, but many chafed under the domination of Rome without reaping the rewards of citizenship. The Roman Senate could impose changes without its allies having a say. A Roman tribune (an elected official) who had attempted to grant citizenship to the allies had been assassinated for his efforts, but in 91 BCE a league of some of the allied cities was formed and broke out in revolt against Rome. There was once again warfare in Italy and large armies marching near to Rome itself.

When this war broke out, two of the outstanding generals were Marius and Sulla. Marius had already been consul several times and won renown in war, while Sulla had earned public acclaim through his leadership in North African campaigns. In the fight against the rebellious Italian cities, Sulla's star rose even higher and, in 88 BCE, he was elected consul for the first time. During his time in office, King Mithridates of Pontus, in Asia Minor, arranged for all Romans in his region to be massacred. Reports suggest that 80,000 men, women and children were killed. Such an insult to Roman pride could not be ignored – war was declared and Sulla was appointed to lead the army against Mithridates.

Marius however had other plans. Through clever manoeuvring he was able to have command of the campaign transferred to him. Sulla could either accept this humiliation or do something no Roman commander had done before, and he did. He marched his army on Rome. There was no force in the city to oppose him, but it is said that the common people reacted by hurling insults and stones at his men. Once in charge of the city, Sulla declared he was simply freeing Rome from tyranny, and had the conduct of the Mithridatic war once again put in his hands.

Almost as soon as Sulla left to attack Mithridates, his enemies in the Senate moved against him. Marius, who had fled the city, returned at the head of another army and took control of Rome for himself. Sulla's allies were driven out or killed on the whim of Marius. Headless bodies were dumped in the streets. Spies searched out any who attempted to conceal themselves. We are told that the streets and roads of all Italy were filled with people fleeing his wrath. Many important senators were put to death after a show trial. Marius died in 86 BCE, but his allies continued to strike at Sulla's power.

In 85 BCE, Sulla concluded a peace treaty with Mithridates and began moving back towards Rome and solidifying his position. When he landed in Italy in 82 BCE, it was at the head of an army which had been hardened in battle against Mithridates. The Romans knew where this was heading – and several commanders immediately transferred their allegiance to Sulla. Despite this, the Romans elected two anti-Sullan candidates to the consulship, including Marius' son, who starting raising forces to oppose Sulla. The armies of the Senate and Sulla met each other at the Battle of the Colline Gate outside of Rome. After a hard-fought clash, Sulla was triumphant and Rome lay at his feet.

THE SETTING SUN

Among Sulla's lieutenants who joined him once he landed in Italy were a number of men who would blaze through Roman history, such as Crassus and Pompey. But being surrounded by brilliant and ambitious young men is not easy. When Pompey demanded a triumph through the streets of Rome to celebrate his victories, Sulla refused him. Pompey, assuming that Sulla was jealous of his popularity, remarked, 'More people worship the rising than the setting sun.' Sulla then allowed the triumph, never guessing quite how high Pompey's sun would rise. When later wondering whether he should march on Rome with his army, Pompey is said to have asked, 'Sulla could do it, why can't I?'

Following the massacre which started his new reign as master of the city, Sulla faced little to no trouble with the usually quarrelsome Senate. He declared himself to be dictator, a position no one had held for over a hundred years.

Sulla began to publish lists of proscriptions. Those who were proscribed were marked for death and their property was to be seized. Anyone who turned in a listed person was rewarded with an enormous sum of gold. Even after paying out lavish amounts to such informers, there was more than enough to swell the treasury.

This was partly because wealthy people were in danger on no other grounds than that their money would be useful to Sulla. A common joke was that men were killed by their large houses or marble baths. One man read his name on the proscription list and remarked, 'My Alban estate is prosecuting me!' However, on the whole, the people sentenced to death were often those who had publicly disagreed with Sulla, or those against whom his followers had private grudges. When people were shocked that Sulla was publishing ever more lists, he simply commented that he was always remembering new enemies of the state.

Even Sulla's friends could not be certain that they were safe. When one of his commanders who had proved useful in the civil war decided to stand for the consulship against Sulla's will, he was killed in the middle of the forum by one of Sulla's officers.

For all the bloodshed, it does seem as if Sulla was attempting to put Rome on a surer foundation than ever before. His reforms of the Roman constitution included setting up new courts to enforce his laws, bringing new blood into the Senate by expanding its membership, and removing the rights of the tribunes (various elected officials) to veto motions. And then, in 80 BCE, with his new Republican order in place, he laid down his dictatorship and retired from Rome.

Having made himself one of the bloodiest tyrants of Rome up until that point, Sulla lived out his last few years in luxury on his country estate writing his memoirs and justifying his actions. He even composed the inscription for his tomb. It is said to have described how no one was ever kinder to his friends, and no one worse to their enemies. Whether Rome would profit from his dictatorship remained to be seen.

JULIUS CAESAR

Gaius Julius Caesar was born in July, 100 BCE (though the month was not called that at the time – it was later renamed after him) into one of the most ancient families in the Roman patrician class. The Julians had lived in Rome for centuries and claimed to be descended from Aeneas, founder of Rome itself, and through him they were direct descendants of the goddess Venus. With a heritage like that, great things were expected of young Gaius.

Caesar's family was fabulously well connected through marriage to many of the most important figures in Roman politics. His aunt was married to the Gaius Marius, who had fought against Sulla (see pages 55). Caesar himself married Cornelia, daughter of one of Sulla's great opponents, but when Sulla took over Rome these connections became dangerous. Sulla ordered Caesar to divorce his wife and retire from positions he had taken – Caesar refused and so had to flee and live in hiding. Sulla was persuaded to forgive Caesar but is said to have commented that in one Caesar there were many Mariuses who might threaten the Republic.

CAESAREAN SECTION?

Many think that Julius Caesar was born by caesarean section, giving the procedure its name. However, such operations were invariably fatal to mothers in antiquity and Caesar's mother is known to have lived for many years after his birth. The name may come from the Latin word *caedere* – meaning 'to cut' – as those cut from mothers that had already died were called *caesones*.

Caesar's rise came through a mix of phenomenal military genius and a deft hand at profiting from the factional fighting and political turmoil which was dividing Rome. Some in the Senate supported the traditional rights of their class, while other politicians stood for election on the side of the people and offered them popular measures of land distribution. In the chaos of the Republican system breaking down, the military commander Pompey, surnamed 'the Great', and Crassus, the wealthiest man in the city, had their own plans on how to fix the state and aggrandize themselves.

When other politicians found ways to stop them individually, they joined together in 60 BCE with Caesar to form a Triumvirate who between them controlled all the levers of power. Crassus and Pompey despised each other and their alliance was mediated by Caesar, who was very much the junior partner between the two great men. With Caesar installed as consul, the Triumvirate passed laws about land reform, made Crassus richer, and ratified Pompey's organization of the provinces in the eastern Mediterranean. Once Caesar's term of office was over, he was granted an army and control of Roman Gaul.

At the time, Rome governed only a small area of modern France on the other side of the Alps from Italy. Caesar was determined to bring the whole of Gaul into the Roman world, and the Gallic wars made Caesar one of the foremost men in the Republic. In a series of campaigns, he drove out invading tribes and destroyed a confederation of groups who opposed him under their leader Vercingetorix. At the Battle of Alesia, Caesar constructed a double wall of siege lines to trap defenders inside a Gaulish settlement and defend his own troops from another attacking army. He also led Roman armies into Britain for the first time, showing that even the most distant lands were not safe from his power.

There is no point in performing these brilliant actions if no one ever hears about them and so Caesar wrote his own dispatches to inform the Roman public of his successes. Alongside these elegant letters, he sent vast amounts of treasure to be paraded through the city. Caesar found himself not only famous but monstrously wealthy and in command of battle-hardened legions. This threatened both the Senate and Pompey and so drove them into each other's arms. Since

Crassus had died, Pompey found that Caesar was now a real rival to his premier position in the Republic. The Senate moved against Caesar and ordered him to abandon his province in Gaul and give up his armies. Caesar refused and marched on Rome, crossing the Rubicon river into Italy in 49 BCE.

Pompey had always boasted that he could summon up enough armies to defend the Republic, but Caesar moved so quickly that the Senate and Pompey were forced to retreat first from Rome and then from Italy. The civil wars had begun. In Rome, Caesar was declared dictator and elected to the consulship before setting out to attack Pompey's forces in the East where they had fled. At the Battle of Pharsalus, Caesar broke the previously undefeated Pompey and scattered his armies. Pompey fled to Egypt, where he was killed, and Caesar simply had to mop up the rest of the resistance to his rule.

Caesar found himself as the only power left in the Republic. Following Pharsalus, Caesar had extended clemency to many of the senators who had opposed him – and this was unforgivable to haughty Roman aristocrats. The senators Caesar pardoned could not pretend that they owed their lives to anything other than the merciful whim of Caesar.

By the end of the civil wars, Caesar had accrued honours that had never been granted to anyone before. Coins were minted with Caesar's face on them. In the Senate, Caesar was granted the right to sit on a golden chair, which his enemies said was nothing less than a throne. It seemed as if Caesar was on course to take on the hated name of king. Instead, he was named dictator for life.

Caesar's reforms of the state may have been designed to stop the degradation of the Republic – which had been happening for decades – but they also drew power and prestige to Caesar himself. Elections were managed to ensure only supporters of Caesar were elected while at the same time keeping the forms of the Republican system in place. Caesar undertook grand building projects. He created a new space where public business could be conducted, the Forum of Caesar, and a new temple to the goddess Venus. Since Caesar claimed descent from Venus, this temple served to glorify Caesar as a near-divine figure.

Caesar had broken the cycle of power-sharing which had mainly ruled the Republic since its foundation. The great

families of the city had shared honours and the positions of power in rotation as a way of stopping any one person becoming monarch. Caesar showed that this could no longer take place: only those in the good books of the dictator could taste glory. A conspiracy was formed by senators who wished to free themselves from his tyranny, including many who had once been pardoned by Caesar. The Republic had been formed when a Brutus drove the last king of Rome out of the city, and a Brutus was at the head of this campaign against Caesar.

On the floor of the Senate, meeting in a theatre constructed by Caesar's enemy Pompey, the conspirators struck on the Ides (15th) of March, 44 BCE. Caesar was planning to set out for a war against the Parthian Empire soon afterwards, so this was the last time they would have an opportunity to move against him.

As Caesar sat on his golden chair in front of the Senate, the conspirators moved in with daggers concealed in their togas. They grabbed the dictator and drove their blades into him in such a frenzy that some of the assassins were themselves injured in the attack. By the time they stopped, Caesar was punctured twenty-three times and lay bleeding to death at the foot of a statue of Pompey. The dictator was dead, but the dictatorship of a single ruler was not quite as dead as it might have seemed. If the conspirators hoped that Caesar's monarchy would end with him then their hopes were soon to be dashed.

Augustus

. . . .

Perhaps the mark of the supreme tyrant is that they never make it publicly known that they are a tyrant. The master of concealing his true position in this regard was the heir of Julius Caesar. Gaius Octavius, better known to history as Augustus, was a great-nephew of Caesar born into a family outside of the patrician rank, without any glorious ancestors to boast of. Yet he survived the bloody end of his great-uncle's rule when Caesar was assassinated, and managed to become the first emperor of Rome – without ever declaring himself as such.

Octavian, as we will call him for now, was born in 63 BCE when Caesar was just another scheming politician in Rome. Nothing great might have been expected of Octavian, and even his mother and stepfather seem to have had little interest in him. But Caesar was impressed when Octavian made a dangerous journey to join his army in Spain when fighting the forces of Pompey. Caesar was so dazzled by Octavian that he named the young man as his primary heir and adopted him as his son. Under Roman law, such adoptions by childless men were common – the result of this adoption was anything but common.

After Caesar's death, Octavian found himself one of the most prominent people in the state and he resolved to fight to claim Caesar's position in Rome. He stole treasury money to raise an army of Caesar's loyalists and stepped directly into the snake pit of Roman politics. Octavian cleverly portrayed himself as the guardian of the Senate; however the Senate entirely misjudged the quality of the man. The statesman Cicero said that they must 'praise him, promote him, and discard him' once he was no longer useful to the Senate. Octavian would not be so easy to discard.

In the political turmoil that followed Caesar's murder, Octavian sided first with the Senate but then joined with Mark Antony and another general called Lepidus to form a Second Triumvirate which took complete control of the state. Caesar had been deified as a god – so Octavian was now known as the son of God. He would not be content to remain as just one of three rulers for long.

To pay for their military adventures, the Triumvirate issued proscription lists which doomed thousands of wealthy and well-connected men to death. To seal the pact between them, each had agreed to sentence one of their own party to execution. Lepidus sacrificed his own brother, Antony his uncle, and Octavian gave up Cicero.

The Roman provinces were sliced up between the new masters of the world. Antony was given the rich East, Lepidus took North Africa, and Octavian claimed Rome and the West. Yet, when power is shared things rarely run smoothly. Antony and Octavian were soon squabbling to be sole ruler as the hapless Lepidus was quickly set aside.

THE APPEARANCE OF SIMPLICITY

As the Emperor Augustus, Octavian was keen to present his family as a model of Roman Republican virtue. His wife Livia was reported to be excellent at spinning and weaving, the skills of a good housewife. Augustus dressed in clothes he claimed were made by the women of his family. Yet it took a lot of staff to give the appearance of such domestic simplicity. A monumental tomb for the slaves belonging to Livia has been discovered with room for over 1,000 burials. Individual inscriptions list slaves and freed people who did Livia's hair and her make-up, or set pearls in her jewellery.

Though Octavian had played his hand superbly well for one of his age, he remained a young man and as prone to missteps as all youths are. During a period of food shortages in Rome, he threw a banquet in which he and his guests dressed up as the gods and gorged themselves. When word of this got out it caused a scandal, and one which Antony was able to use against his supposed partner. Octavian would learn from this that the image of the tyrant must be flawless and in line with public opinion. He also learned how to blacken an opponent's reputation.

When a pretext had to be found for a war against Antony, Octavian knew where to strike.

Around 41 BCE, Antony engaged in a love affair with Cleopatra. Octavian presented this to the Roman public as the rejection of Antony's wife, a pure Roman woman, for an Egyptian witch and enchantress. Antony had already proclaimed that his children by Cleopatra would be named the monarchs of Rome's provinces in the East. His will was taken and read in public and it revealed that Antony wished to be buried in Egypt. Octavian could now present Antony as a foreign enemy worthy of being put down. This was achieved after the Battle of Actium in 31 BCE. Octavian became the only person with real power left in Rome.

Octavian was one of those lucky few people who recognize what they are good at and what they should leave to others. Though the Romans respected military strength, Octavian was no great soldier. He placed his trust in lieutenants to fight his battles. Octavian was more deadly with a stroke of his pen than he ever was with a sword.

Octavian had learned the lessons of his adoptive father well and had no intention of meeting the same fate. Once back in Rome, he was elected to the consulship and promptly handed back control of all the provinces and their armies to the Senate. The Roman Republic of old was being restored, he declared. He himself was nothing more than a simple citizen, he humbly said.

Except everyone was fully aware that there was no one with more authority than Octavian. Even if he held only the ordinary powers of the consul, he was able to call on the armies he had supposedly handed over but who were fully loyal to him. With the wealth he had inherited from Caesar and the booty taken from Antony, there was also no one who could match Octavian financially. The Senate also realized that without Octavian in charge there would simply be another civil war between army commanders who thought they should rule the world. If Octavian was happy to cloak his power in old-fashioned titles, they were happy to turn a blind eye to being under the control of one man.

In 27 BCE, Octavian drew a line under the massacres which had marked his rise to power when he was given the name Augustus by the Senate. This name, which has connotations of being favoured by the gods, was one which would be taken by all the emperors who followed in his place.

Control of most Roman legions was returned to Augustus, supposedly limited to periods of ten years at a time, but in reality for good. For a Roman public tired of endless civil wars, it seemed as if the period with Augustus at the helm of the ship of state was a blessed one. He ushered in an era of peace, celebrated by the erection of a grand monument known as the Ara Pacis Augustae – the Altar of Augustan Peace. Through one of his best friends, the patron of the arts Maecenas, Augustus supported the work of great poets such as Virgil and Horace. In turn, they dutifully churned out verses that honoured the new order which was emerging in Rome.

Augustus ruled Rome for forty years without ever acknowledging the extraordinary position he had crafted for himself. Officially, he was simply the first among equals. When he was on his deathbed in 14 CE, we are told that Augustus asked his friends to applaud his departure from the stage of life if he had played his part well. There have been few tyrants able to play the part of a humble man more ably. When Augustus' will was read, however, it became clear that he intended to hand over his position to his stepson Tiberius. The Romans had entered into an inherited monarchy that would be increasingly hard to disguise.

EMPEROR WENXUAN

The first unification of China under its first emperor, Qin Shi Huang, did not last long. After the death of his son, the political situation devolved once again into several states, now under leaders each claiming to be emperor, warring against each other. In times of turmoil, strong generals often come to hold far more than military power. Gao Huang was one such military strongman.

Gao Huang had served as a lieutenant to a former general who seized power, and had thus learned just how high a successful army commander could rise. He married a princess from the Eastern Wei dynasty that ruled part of north-east China, and had several sons, among whom was Gao Yang, who later became emperor.

Gao Yang was not initially thought to be a promising choice to come to the throne. He was not notably handsome and seemed to be slow to learn things in childhood. Some people laughed at him but others thought there might be the makings of a great man. There were flashes of intelligence which were prompted by his father testing his sons. When they were presented with balls of thread that were hopelessly tangled and commanded to unpick them, while the others struggled with the task Gao Yang simply grabbed a sword and hacked through it. His father thought this very wise, but swords would not always be a good thing in Gao Yang's hands.

As the most powerful general in Eastern Wei, Gao Huang was a kingmaker. In 534 CE, he raised a ten-year-old to the throne, but, as regent, was the real ruler. When he died, his oldest son Gao Cheng took over and began planning to seize the throne for himself before he was stabbed to death by a servant. Gao Yang, despite his supposed stupidity, was not slow to act. He hid the death of his brother and moved his guards into position to seamlessly take over as the power behind the throne.

Gao Yang forced the emperor to pile imperial honours on him. But in 550 CE, after just a year as regent, he tired of the charade of acting under an emperor and 'convinced' the emperor to abdicate in his favour. Gao Yang took the throne as Emperor

Wenxuan of the Northern Qi dynasty, and kindly allowed the former emperor to retire in some style. This kindness lasted only a couple of years before the erstwhile emperor was forced to drink poisoned wine.

At first, Wenxuan was the model of a good emperor. He introduced reforms to make taxation fairer across all levels of society. His army was turned into a fighting force that brought together various ethnic groups to serve under him. While former emperors had been happy to stay in the palace and send out generals to tackle threats, on a number of occasions Wenxuan actually led his soldiers into battle. He saw off invasions and expanded his dominions. Had the course of his reign continued to show this early promise, then Wenxuan might have been remembered as one of the great usurpers in history. There was one great flaw in Wenxuan's character, however.

It seems that Wenxuan had some level of mental instability that was kept under control for the first seven years of his rule. But emperors have access to pretty much everything they want, and what Wenxuan wanted more than anything was alcohol. Being drunk almost all of the time did not help Wenxuan rein in his madness. Some scholars think that he suffered a form of brain damage caused by malnutrition common in alcoholics who stop eating and get most of their calories from alcohol.

Chinese records describe Wenxuan's descent into insanity in vivid detail. It is said the emperor took to drinking all day and singing and dancing at all hours of the day and night.

Sometimes he dressed in barbarian garb, rubbed cosmetics on his face and styled his hair into bizarre fashions during his debauches. Sometimes he simply went without clothes entirely and walked around nude. One of his favourite activities outside of the bottle was riding unlikely animals like elephants, cows and camels. Had this been the limit of his eccentricity then perhaps all would have been well.

Many of the women of the imperial court ended up in the emperor's bed, whether they wished to or not. Wenxuan also enjoyed bringing prostitutes into the palace and forcing his officials to bed them in front of him.

Unfortunately, Wenxuan also had a taste for violence. He was known for wandering around in public carrying a sword and threatening members of the imperial court. One of his

FIRST FLIGHT

In 559 CE, Emperor Wenxuan decided to undertake an experiment in flying. He took a group of condemned prisoners and had them attached to large paper kites and launched from the top of a tower. Most of the experimental subjects plunged to the ground and died, but one man, Yuan Huangtou, is said to have flown two kilometres and landed safely. Unfortunately, the emperor then imprisoned him and had him starved to death.

most shocking attacks came when he attempted to rape the widow of the former emperor, who had also been concubine to his own father. When she resisted him, Wenxuan murdered her with his own hands. He is also known to have stabbed important officials with spears. Wenxuan began to have hallucinations and claimed to see ghosts and hear all manner of strange sounds. These may have driven him to commit further atrocities.

While visiting his wife's home, Wenxuan, predictably, got drunk. He picked up a bow and arrow and shot at his mother-in-law's head. Instead of killing her, he managed to hit her cheek. When this failed to kill her, he set about her with a horsewhip and gave her a hundred lashes.

The emperor's fondness for killing encompassed a number of forms. There was an elegant simplicity to beheading enemies but he also enjoyed burning perceived enemies to death or throwing them into rivers. We are told that the servants of the palace woke up in the morning unsure if they would live until nightfall.

When an emperor is unstable, others have to step in to steady matters. The officials that Wenxuan had hired early in his reign continued to govern effectively when they could. Others had to come up with ways to manage the emperor's outbursts. His most important minister, Yang Yin, thought of a cunning solution to the emperor's habit of killing servants. Prisoners who had been condemned to death already were set to work in the palace, so that if Wenxuan ordered their murder then innocents were not harmed. The prisoners were told that if they were lucky enough to survive three months of this perilous service, they would be set free.

Despite the best efforts of his courtiers, the instability of the emperor could not be concealed, especially when he began targeting his own brothers and burned two to death. With the treasury rapidly dwindling, it became obvious that the state could not afford to be run by a murderous drunkard much longer. Time was against the emperor, anyway. Alcoholism took its toll on his health and he died in 559 CE, passing the throne to a son he had brutalized and left with his own mental issues. This son was in turn deposed by one of Wenxuan's surviving brothers, and the churn of emperors continued.

II

MEDIEVAL HISTORY

WU ZETIAN

Women were not well respected in Chinese society in the seventh century. Confucianism was the dominant school of thought at the time and it had little good to say about women. The philosophy compared them to 'men of base condition' and said that women should act as shadows of the men who governed their lives. No wonder there were no women who ruled China in their own right – none except Wu Zetian.

The sources we have for the remarkable life of Wu Zetian are almost universally hostile to her, as might be expected given her anomalous role as a female ruler. Behind the anecdotes which revel in detailing her villainy, we can catch glimpses of the clever and powerful woman she must have been to take power and hold onto it.

Wu Zetian was not born with the benefits of great wealth or a position at court when she entered the world in 624. She came from a landed family involved in the timber industry, with a tangential relationship to some more important families, but in no way a great dynasty. They did have one house guest who shaped Wu Zetian's life: Li Yuan. Li was a provincial governor who, after leading a successful rebellion, assumed the imperial throne himself as the first ruler of the Tang Dynasty, Emperor Gaozu.

When Gaozu was casting around for concubines for his son Taizong, he summoned fourteen-year-old Wu Zetian to the court. There she impressed people with the unusually comprehensive education which her parents had given her. As a concubine, Wu Zetian did not win favour with Taizong or his wife, but she did start an affair with Taizong's son and heir, who became Emperor Gaozong. Gaozong had not been the most promising of Taizong's children, but after his brothers schemed too obviously to become named as the crown prince, their father disinherited them. Gaozong took the throne, and that should have been the end of Wu Zetian's career.

It was the custom for a deceased emperor's concubines, if they had not produced any sons, to be sent to a monastery. Wu Zetian was accordingly bundled off into seclusion. But while Gaozong was visiting the site to make an offering, he spotted his former mistress and both burst into tears at the reunion. She is said to have prompted the emperor to help her escape from her unwanted religious life by saying that not even he could release her – the subtle attack on his powers caused the emperor to declare that he could do anything he pleased.

Wu Zetian was welcomed by the emperor's wife, who realized that his former lover might be a valuable ally. The emperor was duly happy with Wu Zetian as she soon gave birth to several children. Wu Zetian did not prove to be the friend the empress hoped for, however. When one of Wu Zetian's daughters died, she accused the empress of murder and had her arrested. Some accounts say that the empress was tortured to death on Wu Zetian's orders. Many also claim that Wu Zetian murdered her own daughter to frame the empress for the crime.

In 665, Wu Zetian married Gaozong and was officially made the empress of China. She was not destined to be just an ornament of the court, however, and circumstances demanded that she needed to be something more. Emperor Gaozong was a weak-willed man who was incapable of managing the affairs of state so, dazzled by Wu Zetian's wit and foresight, he relied on her advice. It was said that when the emperor did hold court, Wu sat behind a curtain nearby and whispered the responses he should make into his ear. Then the emperor named one of his sons by Wu Zetian as his heir, and her position in the imperial hierarchy was secured.

It was no good having her son inherit the throne if her husband lost it before he could pass it on, so Empress Wu is said to have employed lethal and ruthless means to protect it. Opponents were demoted and her loyalists moved into position. Those who could not be trusted found themselves charged with crimes and executed. Those who were helpful to Wu Zetian rose high. One loyal supporter became one of the most important officials in the kingdom and was showered with so many rewards that even his infant children came to hold offices of state. The emperor did occasionally attempt to exert his independence from his wife, but she soon put a stop to these outbursts.

Not even the empress' family escaped her alleged murderous machinations. Among those she was blamed for exiling or killing were two of her sons, her brothers, her nephew and her niece. Apparently, the emperor was considering making

FALL AND RISE

When one official suggested the emperor remove Wu Zetian, he was executed along with many members of his family. His granddaughter Shangguan Wan'er was turned into a palace slave. Later, however, her literary talents won her favour with Wu Zetian, who raised her to become her personal secretary. When Shangguan Wan'er was thought to have plotted against her, Wu Zetian spared her from death and merely tattooed her face. In time, however, Shangguan Wan'er was raised to become consort to an emperor.

the niece his consort, but Wu Zetian put a stop to it with the timely application of poisoned food. The emperor's health then worsened, probably caused by a stroke, during which time the empress reigned in all but name for more than twenty years. When he died in 683, Wu Zetian's son became Emperor Zhongzong, but she became his regent.

Emperor Zhongzong showed signs of being rather too independent in wanting to choose officials. Wu Zetian had him removed and forced into exile, and raised another son to the throne as Emperor Ruizong. Ruizong knew his place and only rarely acted to curb the most brutal tactics of his mother's rule. The nobility were not happy at being ruled by a woman – especially one who might kill them at any time – and started a rebellion. When this was crushed, Wu Zetian stopped the charade of being the power behind the throne and had herself officially appointed as the acknowledged ruling monarch of China. Ruizong was probably pleased to be simply demoted to crown prince instead of suffering a worse fate. Empress Wu ruled in her own name from 690 to 705.

During this period, Wu Zetian encouraged people to make secret accusations about others to help her police force detect any potential treason. But, despite the reports of her despotism, many historians find much to praise during her reign. Empress Wu had a knack for spotting talent and appointing the right people to the right office. Her hand-picked generals successfully defended the territory of China and even expanded it. Wu

Zetian also promoted and encouraged the development of Buddhism in China.

Even the most careful and watchful of leaders cannot prevent every plot. In 705, Wu Zetian was ailing and unable to carry the burden of office as she once had, which allowed powerful princes to move against her. Empress Wu was forced to pass the throne to her son, who once again ruled as Emperor Zhongzong. Wu Zetian herself died just a few months later.

Wu was certainly unusual. The steps she took to hold power, however, were not so different from those used by men at this time. If Wu Zetian is viewed less favourably than other great emperors, it may well be because the judgment of history falls hardest on women.

IRENE OF ATHENS

The idea of a woman ruling the Byzantine Empire was not one which any powerful man there ever entertained seriously. For example, when Emperor Heraclius appointed his Empress Martina as regent for his young sons before he died in 641, Martina lasted less than a year in power before her tongue was cut out, her sons were mutilated, and they were forced into exile. Just a century later, however, Irene of Athens would become the first ruling empress of the Byzantine world.

Little is known about the early life of Irene other than that she was born into a well-connected and influential family in Athens in the 750s. The past century had not been a successful one for the Byzantine Empire. Its territory had been chipped away, the Ummayad Caliphate had besieged Constantinople twice, there was religious discord, and emperors rose and fell in quick succession. However, in the late eighth century, the empire was beginning to be stabilized under a new dynasty of emperors, the Isaurian, and the young co-emperor Leo IV was on the search for a bride. For reasons that are unclear, in 769 Irene of Athens was chosen.

The new dynasty had, however, created internal strife as the emperors backed the cause of iconoclasm – the destruction of religious icons venerated by many Byzantine Christians.

Most of the chroniclers of history in the Byzantine empire came from monastic communities which had been raided and attacked by Imperial agents destroying the icons, and these historians therefore treated several emperors harshly in their accounts. Due to his iconoclastic activities, Leo IV's father was described as having bathed in the blood of Christians and to have been as bad as any ancient pagan tyrant. Leo IV was more moderate – when it suited him – but was not above torturing members of his own court when he found them with icons.

Irene seems to have been secretly fond of icons and tried to conceal her beliefs, but not well enough. When the emperor discovered two icons hidden in her pillow, he rebuked her and is said to have refused to sleep with her anymore. Her position was more secure than most, however, as she had given birth to Leo's son and heir, who was crowned as co-emperor in 776 at the age of just five. Irene would not have to live in fear of her husband for long. He died in 780 and Irene became regent for her young son Constantine VI.

Within weeks of becoming regent, Irene was forced to put down a conspiracy to oust her son by Leo IV's brothers who believed one of their number, Nikophoros, would make a better emperor. Irene was able to capture all those involved. The royal uncles were forced to become priests, which meant they were ineligible to become emperor, and any official who had sided with them was removed and replaced with men loyal to her. Irene had secured the throne for her son, and for herself.

POISONED CROWN

The death of Leo IV was said to have been caused by his lust for gemstones. When he took a bejewelled crown from a church where it had been dedicated by a former emperor, he is said to have placed it on his head – and contracted a fever for his impiety. The story may have been spread by Irene herself to blacken her husband's reputation and she certainly made a great show of returning the crown to its rightful home after his death.

Irene was not content to be a power behind the throne. She took steps to ensure that everyone was aware that she was in charge of affairs. Her coins call her the co-ruler of the empire and show her, not her son, holding an orb of power. Irene continued her policy of dealing with suspected traitors swiftly. When a general was reported to be a supporter of Nikophoros, she sent a fleet to capture him, and had his wife and children whipped and imprisoned. The regent also reversed iconoclasm throughout the empire, which caused friction with many in the church and at court. Irene preferred to raise to positions of authority eunuchs, who would obey only her, rather than trusting members of important families who might have conflicting loyalties.

Young emperors do not stay young, however, and Constantine VI eventually reached the age when he should have been ruling on his own, but his mother showed no signs of stepping aside. In 790, he began recruiting supporters to oust Irene, but one of her eunuchs uncovered the clandestine plot and Constantine was placed under house arrest. Irene claimed to have received divine signs that the empire should be hers and attempted to make the army give an oath to follow her alone, but many soldiers refused to be led by an empress. Irene was forced to step down and Constantine VI was placed on the throne in reality for the first time.

Constantine showed leniency to his mother and allowed her to remain at court. But his attempts to win a military victory which would bolster his authority ended in a shambles, and some nobles once again considered making Nikophoros the emperor. However, Constantine had learned from Irene what to do with traitors: he had Nikophoros blinded and the tongues of his other uncles torn out – no mutilated man was allowed to rule. Constantine's popularity continued to plunge when he divorced his well-liked wife, who had failed to give him a son, to wed one of his mistresses.

Irene was watching.

Irene stoked the flames of discontent against her own son by encouraging religious authorities to speak out against his actions. She had also managed to place her powerful eunuchs back in control of many of the key offices of state. In 797, she was ready to strike. Constantine VI was captured by his mother's agents and his eyes cut out. It is thought unlikely that he survived this torture and he disappears from history at this point. Even for the Byzantines, this was a cut-throat action. It was reported that a mother blinding her own son was so diabolical that God darkened the skies for several days. Whatever the divine opinion, Irene was now the sole ruler of the Byzantine world.

A ruling empress was not something many could accept in Europe at the time. For the first time since antiquity, the throne of the Roman empire was not occupied by a man – and nature abhors a vacuum. In 800, Charlemagne, king of the Franks, was crowned as the new Roman emperor by the pope. This was a direct attack on the prestige of the Byzantines, who considered themselves the sole heirs to Rome.

Irene managed to hold onto her position for only four years before her own finance minister engineered a plot to bring her down. For all her scheming, Irene could not see off this last conspiracy and she was exiled to a small island in 802 where she is said to have had to earn her living spinning wool. She did not have to labour for long. She died just one year after being removed as the first ruling empress in Europe.

ANDRONIKOS I KOMNENOS

The Byzantine Empire suffered several crises in the tenth and eleventh centuries. The economy was tottering, the emperors were weak in the face of powerful nobles and officials, and the empire was attacked on several fronts. In 1057, a general called Isaac Komnenos rose up against Emperor Michael VI and deposed him, becoming the first ruler of the Komnenos dynasty. The Byzantine empire under the Komnenos emperors managed to rebuild some stability – but it could not shake off the tendency for family members to connive against each other.

Andronikos Komnenos was born into the imperial family around 1120. Although he was a grandson of Emperor Alexios I Komnenos, he did not have any direct line to the throne. He was tall, strong, handsome, knew how to wield a sword and could be excellent company with his witty and intelligent conversation. He also seems to have had the one indispensable attribute of the would-be ruler – he was ambitious.

At first, Andronikos proved to be a loyal servant to his cousin, the Emperor Manuel I Komnenos, who was more like a brother to him. Manuel may have enjoyed spending time with Andronikos but he knew better than to entrust him with important positions at court as Andronikos was often sloppy with his duties. Manuel did put Andronikos in charge of an army to recapture some territory that had been taken from the empire, but Andronikos failed to regain the lands. Despite this, and even though there were rumours that Andronikos was plotting to usurp the throne, he was allowed to remain at court, where he promptly started an incestuous affair with one of his cousins.

When Andronikos made treasonous overtures to the Hungarians in hopes of them lending him an army to seize the throne, Manuel had to act. He imprisoned his wayward cousin in a dank cell beneath the palace. For all of his other faults, Andronikos was tenacious. He is reported to have escaped his cell several times.

In one case, Andronikos dug into the bare earth of his cell and discovered a disused tunnel where he concealed himself. Thinking that he had escaped, Manuel had Andronikos' wife arrested and sent to the same cell in his place. As darkness fell, Andronikos emerged and is said to have conceived his son that night. Eventually, Andronikos was recaptured.

After another escape attempt, he was captured by soldiers who determined to return him to the emperor. The wily Andronikos told his captors he was suffering from a bout of dysentery and so had to stop several times a day to empty his bowels. On one such occasion, after disappearing behind a bush, he placed his hat atop a pole so it would look like he was still there and slipped away. Making his way to an enemy court, Andronikos tried yet again to raise forces to make himself emperor. He failed, but time seemed to be on his side – Manuel had reigned for twenty years without producing an heir. Then in 1169, Manuel's son Alexios was born, at which point it became clear that Andronikos was slipping further from his goal. Running out of places to hide, Andronikos returned to Constantinople and begged Manuel for forgiveness. He was granted a province to govern and might have lived in quiet luxury, but in 1180 an opportunity arose when eleven-year-old Alexios II became emperor after his father's death, with his mother as his regent.

Things went wrong for the young emperor immediately. His mother and her reputed lover made unpopular deals with Italian merchants and were thought to be squandering the treasury. The Latins, as Western Europeans were known, were perceived as greedy, arrogant and dirty by the Byzantines. Worse was that the regents allowed neighbouring nations to raid across the border. Riots in the streets gave Andronikos his chance.

In 1182, Andronikos marched to the capital with an army and was greeted rapturously by the populace as the saviour of the young emperor. One of Andronikos' first actions was to attack the Latin ships in the harbour, while a mob stormed their homes and massacred the men, women and children they found there. When a representative of the pope was discovered, his head was hacked off and dragged through the streets by dogs.

Andronikos struck at the regent's supporters by claiming that he only had good intentions for Alexios II. The emperor's mother was bundled into a monastery and later poisoned. Andronikos' own sister and her influential husband were also killed. When a group of nobles attempted to stop Andronikos they were all captured and blinded. Andronikos was later called *misophaes* – the hater of sunlight – by his enemies because so many people were blinded at his command.

In 1183, Andronikos was proclaimed as joint emperor with Alexios by supporters who said a strong man was needed to defend the empire against invaders. Shortly afterwards, Alexios simply disappeared and Andronikos became the sole emperor.

To shore up his throne, the sixty-something Andronikos married Alexios' thirteen-year-old widow. He was lecherous, having carried out affairs throughout his life, and when his physical body could not keep up with his lusty will he turned to aphrodisiacs made from the rarest and costliest ingredients.

Byzantine historians who wrote about Andronikos' reign were all hostile to him and were probably influenced by their noble patrons, whose worst abuses Andronikos attempted to curb. He also tried to reform the tax system to make even the mightiest aristocrats pay their share. However, he brutally suppressed opposition and would round up his enemies using false – or secret – accusations. Many nobles found that they were safer abroad than at home.

In 1185, these nobles found support from the ruler of Sicily, who gave them the forces to launch an invasion. At the same time, Andronikos attempted to arrest one of his relatives, Isaac, who was suspected of treason. Isaac cleaved the head off the man sent to capture him and brandished the bloody blade as he rode to the great church of Hagia Sophia to seek sanctuary. The people took this as a sign to rise up against Andronikos, and Isaac was crowned as the new emperor.

Facing internal and external strife, Andronikos was unable to stop his inevitable downfall. He was reduced to personally firing arrows into the crowds attacking his palace. When this proved ineffective, he tried to escape the city in a small boat but was soon captured and given to the mercy of the crowd. They mutilated him over several days before tying a rope around his battered corpse and hanging it upside down for all to revile.

GENGHIS KHAN

If you visit Ulaanbaatar, capital of Mongolia, you will likely fly into Chinggis Khaan airport. You might meet students studying at Chinggis Khaan university. For a day trip you might want to visit the world's largest equestrian statue – a glittering

steel sculpture of Chinggis Khaan which stands watch over the Mongolian steppes. Known in English as Genghis Khan, to Mongolians he is a national hero, but many other nations consider him one of the deadliest tyrants to burst out of central Asia. Tracking down the real Genghis Khan among these various interpretations can be difficult.

The man who would found the Mongol Empire which, at its greatest extent, stretched from the eastern shores of China to the gates of Vienna, was born as Temüjin in 1162. At the time, the horse-riding tribes of Mongolia were split into a great number of rival clans. While Temüjin was the son of a tribal leader, later accounts suggested that his mother had been made pregnant by a shining beam of light. Destiny was said to be on Temüjin's side from birth as he emerged from his mother's womb clutching a blood clot in his tiny fingers, which presaged his bloody conquests.

While his rise might have been fated, it was not to be an easy ascent to the pinnacle of power. His father died when Temüjin was just nine years old, and the confederation of clans gathered by his father fractured at once. Temüjin's mother Hö'elün attempted to hold the people together for her sons and stepsons but she was ignored and the family was forced to scrabble in the wilds for survival. The brothers were left to fight over tiny fish they caught in a stream and Hö'elün had to remind them to work together as they had no friends and only their shadows for company.

It is impossible here to condense the tale of how Temüjin became paramount leader of the Mongols. It was a twisted path of alliances, betrayals, battles and executions. But by 1206, Temüjin had all of the tribes under his control and summoned them to a meeting where he was officially named as Genghis Khan (which probably means 'Universal Ruler') – sole ruler of his people. He had big plans for his hundreds of thousands of followers, and the Mongols would have to change if they were to live up to his lofty ambitions.

The tribes of the Mongols existed as mobile groups who migrated regularly across the grassy plains of their territory. Genghis Khan would have to form them into a more united whole to forge an empire. Over the course of his reign, he adopted the use of a written language and created a system of couriers to carry his messages across his realm. A law code was developed to simplify justice. The warriors who had formerly been loyal to their own tribal leaders now swore allegiance to the Great Khan. It was time for the Mongols to look beyond their own borders.

Like many medieval rulers, Genghis Khan knew the importance of being open-handed with gifts to his followers. By waging wars that brought in vast quantities of gold, silver, luxuries and land, he had plenty of rewards to hand out.

His first target was the Jin kingdom of northern China, whose emperors had been used to dealing with fragmented tribes of Mongols and even collected tribute from them. The Mongol army was superbly adapted to lightning swift campaigns given their reliance on cavalry and their traditions of carrying all necessary supplies with them. In 1211, the Mongols smashed into China with tens of thousands of men. Despite being heavily outnumbered and suffering several defeats, the unified Mongols broke through Chinese defences. The Mongols would attack a city, devastate it, and then retreat before Chinese forces could counter-attack. Destroying cities acted as a warning to others not to offer even token resistance. Eventually, they surrounded the capital. The Mongols were finally bought off with booty and an imperial princess to become one of Genghis Khan's many wives. This state of peace did not last and the Mongols continued to press deeper into Chinese territory, capturing cities as they went.

Genghis Khan then turned his attentions westwards towards the Qara Khitai empire which covered large areas of central Asia. The Qara Khitai people had been ruled by an erstwhile Chinese dynasty for nearly a hundred years but they had recently been taken over by a usurper called Kuchlug. Kuchlug had adopted Buddhism as his faith and tried to force his mostly Muslim subjects to do the same – going so far as to crucify an imam. Unlike this intolerance, Genghis Khan had a policy of allowing his subjects to worship who they liked, so long as they remained loyal to him. Realizing that Kuchlug's religious intolerance had lost him the support of many of his subjects, the Mongols invaded. Kuchlug's head was cut off and carried across his former kingdom to show that the former ruler was dead.

HOW TO LOSE AN EMPIRE

When faced with an overture of trade by one of history's great conquerors, it is probably wise to treat the merchants politely. However, the shah of the Khwarazmian Empire, which bordered the Qara Khitai, seized a Mongol trade caravan in 1218 and then beheaded ambassadors sent by Genghis Khan. The Mongols invaded in 1219 and destroyed the empire, supposedly killing millions of victims into the bargain.

The Mongols now ruled land from northern China to the Caspian Sea. The armies of Genghis Khan raided as far as Kiev and into Iran. Several of the wealthiest cities in the world in this region were besieged by the Mongols and, if they resisted, utterly annihilated. The city of Nishapur, which made the mistake of killing a high-ranking Mongol, was systematically wiped out in a few days in 1221. Every resident of the city of hundreds of thousands was beheaded.

In 1221, Genghis Khan was forced to turn back towards his homelands to deal with rebellions that had sprung up at his rear. To forestall future resistance, he developed a complex governmental system which would see the khan placing governors and officials over conquered peoples. The Xia dynasty of western China had failed to provide the Mongols with support when called on, and so, in 1225, he led an army against them. The Xia were no match for the Mongols and Genghis was well on the way to seizing their land when illness overtook him.

Genghis Khan died in his tent in 1227 but the fact of his death was hidden until the Mongols captured the capital of the Xia. The secrecy allowed legends to accrue about the nature of his demise. Some said he was struck by divine lightning, others that he was injured during the siege, yet another that one of Genghis' concubines stabbed him in the genitals during sex. However it happened, in the wake of his death the Xia were wiped out for defying the great Great Khan. Little knowledge remains of them today, while all the world knows the name of Genghis Khan.

Genghis Khan was buried with great splendour in Mongolia at a site which has since been forgotten. Marco Polo said that he was buried along with 2,000 slaves who buried him, and the soldiers who guarded them were also slain to ensure no one knew where he lay. The Mongol Empire continued to grow under the rule of Genghis' son Ögedei.

The cultural change caused by the sudden rise of the Mongol Empire may have been matched by wider effects on the planet. Some studies suggest that the reduction in population caused by Genghis' invasions, and the reforestation of lands left fallow, may have contributed to a cooling of the planet.

NARATHIHAPATE

. . . .

Every monarch wants to go down in history with an impressive epithet. They dream of being remembered as 'the Wise', 'the Good' or 'the Great'. Unfortunately, they do not get to choose, so they are just as likely to be ranked alongside Childeric the Idiot, Henry the Impotent, or any number of those called 'the Fat'. Narathihapate, of the Burmese kingdom Pagan (also called Baggan), is destined to be known forever as Taruk-Pyay Min – 'the king who fled from the Mongols'.

Narathihapate was the son of Crown Prince Uzana of Pagan, but his mother was a commoner and so he was not expected to inherit the throne. Instead, that was destined for his half-brother Thihathu, who was publicly anointed as the heir after their father became king.

When Uzana unwisely went out elephant hunting, however, the fate of the kingdom shifted. Uzana attempted to kill a wild elephant but it gored the elephant the king was riding on and in the collapse of the royal mount, Uzana was killed. Thihathu was on the point of being declared the new king when a group of ministers, led by Yazathingyan, decided to make a change to the line of succession. Yazathingyan told the other ministers that Thihathu was a proud man who would make the people suffer. Worse, he had once spat red betel juice on Yazathingyan. Why not place the crown on Narathihapate? At just eighteen years old he would be much easier to control. Thihathu was duly taken prisoner and disappeared from the historical record while Narathihapate became king in 1254.

Despite their hopes that Narathihapate would be a biddable young king, the advisors who had planned to control him found him to be unpredictable, for example when he raised low-born people to positions of high authority. Yazathingyan attempted to shame the king by taking a broken bowl to the palace and eating from it. When Narathihapate was puzzled by this, the minister explained that since all of the workers were now government officials there was no one left to make new bowls. His subtle prodding only earned Yazathingyan a sentence of exile.

The king found that he could not rule without experienced men around him when two of his vassals rose up in rebellion in 1258. Narathihapate was forced to recall Yazathingyan to lead his armies to suppress the revolts. When Yazathingyan and his sons settled the dangers to his rule, Narathihapate was happy to reward them richly. Unfortunately, Yazathingyan died soon afterwards and the reign of Narathihapate descended into tragic farce.

The accounts of this period, known as *The Glass Palace Chronicles*, tell us that Narathihapate was an ogre and filled with monstrous appetites. When he sat down to dinner he was never satisfied unless there were at least 300 dishes set on his table. It is said that the king kept 3,000 concubines to satisfy his sexual desires. Narathihapate was described as extremely covetous, given to outbursts of wrath, and haughtier than even a king should be.

No one likes becoming ill but Narathihapate took his fear of sickness to murderous lengths. It was death to sneeze in his presence, and even a yawn could mean death. Some said that Narathihapate was simply too blessed to sneeze or yawn himself and so did not understand that mere mortals often do both. Dogs, however, were allowed to sneeze. When one did so under his dinner table, the king offered it a portion of his dinner. This proved to be lucky for him as his queen had put poison in Narathihapate's meal as revenge for a practical joke which saw her being splashed with water. The dog died and the queen's plot was discovered. She was burned to death.

Narathihapate was not notably pious but he did spend lavishly on religious objects and rituals. His most famous outlay of cash was on the creation of a vast, and vastly expensive, temple known as the Mingalazedi Pagoda. He is said to have cast large statues in pure gold and silver, decorating them with the most extraordinary jewels. He had a costly reliquary made for relics of the Buddha and instead of depositing it simply in his temple, he had it carried there on a white elephant accompanied by hundreds of royal officials each decked out in expensive jewellery. The king was not one to be modest, and he declared in an inscription in the pagoda that he could call on thirty-eight million warriors. The problem was that the treasury was being rapidly depleted by Narathihapate's spending and inability to bring in taxes, and while he boasted of his huge armies, they did not actually exist.

SLOW CONSTRUCTION

A prophecy was put about that as soon as the Mingalazedi Pagoda was finished the kingdom would fall into ruin. Understandably, Narathihapate decided to take his time in completing the work and dragged his feet for six years. A holy man visited the king and convinced him that clinging to his kingdom out of fear was irreligious and the pagoda was worth the risk. Whether this was so, history would be the judge.

This might not have been a problem if Narathihapate had lived in a peaceful era, but to his northern border there was the Yuan Dynasty of Mongols ruling in China. They sent Narathihapate a series of demands for both tribute and aid against their enemies. Narathihapate was not willing to acquiesce to either of these. The Chinese envoys failed to show the proper respect that Narathihapate expected and he ordered them and the thousand horsemen accompanying them to be slain. This did not go down well with the Yuan.

In 1277, the Mongols, under the command of Kublai Khan, invaded and the Pagan empire began to fall apart. Vassal states were conquered by the Yuan, and Narathihapate was forced to retreat from his capital towards the south. All of his riches were loaded into boats and floated down the river to safety, but when it became clear that there was not enough room for all of his female slaves he ordered them to be bound and thrown into the river as he did not want them to be captured by the Chinese. This mass murder was only avoided by the advice of an official.

Narathihapate had three sons whom he had placed in control of important cities, but he found that he could not trust them. Moreover, each plotted against the others. As much of his kingdom had fallen and he could not rely on his own family for support, Narathihapate decided that peace with the Yuan could be his salvation. In 1286, Narathihapate agreed to complete submission to Kublai Khan and sent envoys to the Chinese court to ratify the peace.

Alas, Narathihapate was not to be saved. One of his own sons captured him and gave him the choice between taking poison or being stabbed to death. Narathihapate chose the poison and died. With him died the Pagan empire, as his sons never managed to restore the land which had been lost.

RICHARD III

A wicked uncle who steals a throne and murders his young, innocent nephews. This is the stuff of fairy tales. But there are few more infamous kings in English history than the crook-backed Richard III, and he has been cast as the archetype of

this evil trope. His position as the most monstrous of rulers was cemented by William Shakespeare's play which presents Richard as the eloquent face of villainy:

'To entertain these fair well-spoken days,
I am determined to prove a villain
And hate the idle pleasures of these days.
Plots have I laid, inductions dangerous …'

Richard III, Act 1, Scene 1

Though everyone thinks they know the true story of Richard III and his usurpation of the throne, there is still a great deal of debate about how tyrannical his rule was.

Richard was born in 1452 into an England facing crisis. His father, Richard, Duke of York, was one of the greatest lords in the realm and believed he had a better claim to the throne than the ruling Henry VI. The king was notably pious but prayers alone do not secure the crown. Henry VI was weak in war, vacillating in politics and mentally unstable. Following the catastrophic loss of most English lands in France, the king fell into catatonic withdrawal and was completely unable to take part in government of his kingdom. Even the birth of a son and heir could not induce Henry to respond to life. The Duke of York became the protector of the realm. However, this did not settle the growing rivalries between the great houses struggling to seize power from their failing monarch.

It has been said that Henry VI's madness was a tragedy, but when he recovered his sanity in 1454, it was a national disaster. Once back in power, he undid all of Richard's work and set the stage for a military confrontation. In 1459, a civil war erupted with Richard leading Yorkist forces against those loyal to the king, the Lancastrians. This was the start of the Wars of the Roses.

Richard, Duke of York, was slain in the Battle of Wakefield the following year but his claim to the throne was carried on by his oldest son Edward, and the future Richard III would fight by Edward's side in the wars to come. Henry VI was deposed in 1461 and Edward IV was crowned in his place. With his brother's elevation, Richard became the Duke of Gloucester and amassed lands and important positions. But sitting on a throne does not mean you cannot be toppled from it. The Lancastrians rebelled and, in 1470, Edward was forced into exile. Henry VI was proclaimed king again, but was once more unable to rule on his own. He could barely walk without being supported. Edward returned with foreign aid in 1471 to take back his throne and Henry VI was captured, disappeared into the Tower of London and quietly – and helpfully – died.

Richard was loyal to Edward IV, served him as a general, and provided a huge number of men as well as money to regain the throne for his family. Their brother George, Duke of Clarence, however, had changed sides several times and caused havoc for the family. Though George had returned to the fold

DISABILITY AND DISCOVERY

Richard III was painted by Shakespeare and other writers as being severely disabled, which at the time was thought to be a mark of moral failings. He was described as having a withered arm, twisted spine and hump on his back, yet he was also thought to be a skilled warrior on the battlefield. It was only when his remains were discovered in 2012 under a car park in the city of Leicester that the truth became clear. Richard did suffer from scoliosis which may well have given him one shoulder higher than the other, but he seems to have not let it hold him back from riding into battle and wielding a sword.

he continued to cause trouble. In 1477, he was arrested and charged with treason for violating the prerogatives of the king and interfering with justice. He was put to death in the Tower, supposedly drowned in a vat of Malmsey wine on Richard's orders. Was this part of Richard's plan to clear his way to the throne?

Richard might have felt entitled to the throne as Edward IV had made one of the most surprising marital matches in royal history. Instead of marrying an important princess or daughter of a great magnate, he chose Elizabeth Woodville, a widow with two surviving sons whose first husband fought against Edward. The marriage was carried out in secret and

Elizabeth was suddenly presented to the court as the queen, to the shock of many. The new queen's relatives soon dominated the court and created friction with many of the older noble families.

Edward IV died suddenly in 1483 and left two young sons, Edward and George. His lineage should have been secure. But a child cannot rule, and so the new Edward V was placed under the protection of his uncle Richard. One of Elizabeth's brothers had been guarding the king, but Richard had him arrested and executed for treason. Elizabeth fled with several of her children to seek sanctuary in Westminster Abbey while Edward V and his brother were moved to the Tower of London, to await the coronation on 22 June – it would never come.

Few people visited the young king, for the true power in the realm was Richard. This situation could not last. At a council meeting, Richard had Lord Hastings – the powerful Lord Chamberlain – arrested and killed for supposed treachery against him. On the day of the planned coronation, a preacher named Ralph Shaa delivered a sermon on the Biblical verse 'Bastard slips shall never take deep root', and revealed that Edward IV and Elizabeth were never legitimately married. So, the princes Edward and George were illegitimate. To further muddy the waters, Edward IV was himself accused of being illegitimate. Only Richard, it was claimed, was the true son of the old Duke of York and so only he had a rightful claim to the throne, which he soon took as Richard III.

The Princes in the Tower, as the young former king and his brother became known, were moved to more private quarters in the Tower and slowly disappeared from sight. No one can say what happened to them, but they were never seen alive after the summer of 1483 and their bodies have never been recovered. The wicked uncle was the only legitimate male member of his family left alive.

Few people love a usurper and neither those who had supported Henry VI nor those who had fought for Edward IV had reason to stay loyal to Richard III. Even his close ally the Duke of Buckingham raised a rebellion against Richard. This proved to be a debacle and Buckingham was soon captured and executed. However, there was another threat to Richard's rule, and it was lurking in France.

The Duke of Buckingham had intended to replace Richard III with Henry Tudor, who was related to the former royal house of Lancaster and had spent more than a decade in exile in France. The end of Buckingham's revolt did not end Henry Tudor's desire to be king. With French backing, as well as the support of many nobles and the Woodvilles, Henry invaded in 1485.

At the Battle of Bosworth, the armies of Richard and Henry met. Richard III's force was numerically superior but as the battle ebbed and flowed Richard III made a brave and desperate charge directly at Henry Tudor. Had he succeeded in bringing Henry down then the rebellion would have died with him. Instead, Richard III was struck down from his horse and viciously butchered. His corpse was stripped and carried away for burial on a farm cart. Henry went in triumph to London to become the founder of the Tudor dynasty.

YEONSANGUN OF JOSEON

It is always dangerous to give a young person so much power that they do not conceive of their subjects as fully human. The Roman emperor Caligula came to the throne at the age of twenty-four and said, 'Remember, I have the right to do anything to anybody.' Yeonsangun became king of Joseon in Korea in 1494 even younger than Caligula, aged just eighteen, and his childhood had already been bloody enough to unsettle anyone's mental stability.

The reign of Yeonsangun's father had been stable and prosperous for his kingdom, but not so for his family life. The king's first wife had died suddenly and so he raised his concubine, Lady Yun, to become his queen, and she bore him Prince Yeonsangun, the heir to the throne. Queen Yun had therefore fulfilled her dynastic responsibilities and should have been secure in her position, living a life of honoured privilege, but she seemed temperamentally unsuited to be a queen.

As Yun had been a concubine raised to the throne, she viewed the remaining concubines as potential threats to her position. She was accused of poisoning one of the women of the court and lost favour with her husband. A faction at the court, perhaps sensing that they could place a lady more favourable to their aims on the throne, convinced the king that execution was the only fit punishment for Yun and so she was put to death by poison. The king selected Jeonghyeon as his new bride – although many thought her family was responsible for the previous queen's downfall. Prince Yeonsangun, still a toddler at the time, was raised to believe the new queen was his mother.

It is commonly said that a child who shows cruelty to animals will progress to cruelty towards humans as an adult. Yeonsangun was walking through the palace gardens one day when a tame deer approached and happened to mark his sleeve with its nose. The prince responded by giving the deer a painful kick. He was told off for this casual brutality, but he never forgot his hatred of the deer. Once he became king, he stabbed it with a spear.

When his father died in 1494, Yeonsangun ascended to the throne and, according to most historians, his reign began as one of stability and reverence for tradition. Perhaps the young king chafed under the guidance and control of the ministers around him, however, and looked for ways to free himself of their influence. This chance came when Yeonsangun learned the truth about his real mother's death, at which point the king unleashed a wave of retribution against many members of the court who had been around at the time. The executions which followed could be bloody affairs with people torn limb from limb or beaten to death. Even the dead could not escape punishment, with their tombs raided and their corpses mutilated.

The ideal of kingship at this time was that of a just, powerful scholar. The Joseon court had various factions and one of the most powerful was that of the scholars who controlled many of the positions of power and so could curtail the king's actions. There was also a unique account of the reigns of the Joseon kings in the form of official daily records kept by historians. However, from his youngest days Yeonsangun had never cared for academics, and treated them as his enemies once he became king. He converted the important Seonggyungwan centre of learning into his personal pleasure palace and brothel, ignoring the scholars who came and wailed outside the gates. The official records were then turned against their authors and subjects, since Yeonsangun consulted the books to find evidence for anyone he decided to execute as a traitor. After Yeonsangun's reign, the kings were no longer given access to the records to prevent this ever happening again.

Yeonsangun unleashed two major campaigns against scholars, which became known as the Literati Purges. During the First Literati Purge, when Yeonsangun found an excuse to attack the scholars, some of them were exiled, some were beheaded, but some were sentenced to death by *lingchi* – execution by a slow series of cuts which removed flesh piece by piece.

The Second Literati Purge came after the king was given a piece of clothing that was said to be covered in the vomit his mother coughed up after she was poisoned. This reminder of his mother's death opened the door to further executions. More members of the scholars' party were killed, but so were members of the opposing political faction whom the king blamed for not protecting his mother. No one was safe. Dowager Queen Jeonghyeon, who had raised the king as her own son, was met outside her chamber by men with drawn swords. Only the prompt action of Yeonsangun's own wife saved the dowager's life. By acting against the scholars, Yeonsangun removed the last checks to his rule.

The king then descended into drunken revelry with his close male companions. They were often found stumbling around the palace or comatose after long bouts of indulgence. To supply women for the king's bed, teams were sent out to seize the most attractive girls from across the country and drag them back to the palace. King Yeonsangun was so notorious for debauching pretty girls that some came up with clever ploys to repel him. One kept pieces of rotting meat around and when summoned to the palace placed them in her armpits so that she reeked and the king sent her home.

OH DEER

The official historians were meant to be legally protected from retribution by the king, to ensure the honest reporting of events. This led to kings sometimes attempting to hide embarrassing events from the historians before they could write them down. When the earlier King Taejong fell from his horse during a deer hunt, he was heard to mutter, 'Do not let the historians know about this.' Fortunately, the historians did hear this – and entered both the accident and his comment into the annals.

When members of the court dared to question his actions, King Yeonsangun would remove the officials and abolish the offices they held to stop others following in their footsteps. Those who survived had to wear plaques with a warning not to let their tongues wag so much that they would end up having their heads cut off. When you are the king, however, your misdemeanours cannot be hidden inside the court forever.

Letters complaining about the king's crimes were anonymously delivered to the court. When presented with them, the king ordered the gates of the capital to be closed and the culprits discovered. The authors were not found, so King Yeonsangun ordered the complete suppression of the *Hangul* writing script in which the letters were written. Anyone who used *Hangul* was sentenced to death and anyone who failed to turn in their neighbours who knew how to write it were given a hundred blows with a stick.

By 1506, the people were unhappy with their ruler, court officials were scared for their lives, and the nobles resented the king's interference in their traditional rights. A coup was launched which saw Yeonsangun deposed from his throne and replaced with one of his half-brothers. Yeonsangun was banished to a distant island where he could harm no one.

His exile did not last long as within the year he was dead. At court, Yeonsangun's wife was put to death and all of his sons were executed to ensure that the new king could not be challenged.

III

Early Modern History

Ludovico Sforza

Italy in the fifteenth century was at the forefront of the cultural flourishing known as the European Renaissance. New heights were being reached in the arts and literature by some of the great minds of the day. This was only possible because there was no Italy at the time. Italy as we know it now was then a patchwork of states such as the Kingdom of Naples, the Republic of Florence and the Papal States. Each of these patronized artists to glorify themselves. But the battle between the states was military and political as well as artistic.

The Sforza family ruled the Duchy of Milan after Francesco Sforza, a *condotierro*, or leader of one of the mercenary bands common in Italy at the time, took control of it in 1450.

Ludovico Sforza was Francesco's fourth surviving son and so had no real prospects of becoming the duke.

On the death of his father in 1466, Ludovico became the Count of Mortara, while his brother Galeazzo became the next Duke of Milan. Since Galeazzo was still a young man, he relied on his mother, Bianca Visconti, to support his rule, but being a duke does not always lend itself to close family ties. When she tried to steer his conduct away from chasing women and money and towards good governance, Galeazzo sent Bianca into exile.

The court of Milan at this time was a suitably splendid place to befit a Renaissance prince. Artists were attracted from across Europe to beautify the city. While Galeazzo was popular with the people on the streets, there was grumbling among the wealthier elements of the city. The duke had made a number of enemies thanks to various rulings which angered some, and his dishonourable seduction of women, which angered more. One of these disgruntled noblemen was Andrea Lumpugnani, who had been pardoned for a crime by Galeazzo's father but hated the current duke for refusing to grant him rights to land he desired. He and his allies decided that the only solution was to rid themselves of Galeazzo.

On 26 December 1476, they waited for Galeazzo in a church. Lumpugnani greeted the duke by falling to his knees in front of him and seemingly asking forgiveness – then he struck upwards with a dagger, bringing Galeazzo to the ground. The other assassins joined in and slaughtered the duke. The others made a swift escape but Lumpugnani stumbled, which slowed him enough that he was caught and quickly killed in turn. The assassins may have hoped the city would rise to support them but they were soon disappointed. The Sforza line was to be continued by Galeazzo's son Gian, then still a minor.

A child ruler is always an opportunity for a would-be usurper, and soon all of Galeazzo's brothers, including Ludovico, descended on the city to insist on their right to act as regent for the young man in place of his mother, Bona. When their attempts failed, they were sent into exile. But in 1479, Ludovico raised an army, marched on Milan, drove out the regent's advisors and assumed a position of power in the city. He did not yet have complete control, as Bona's lover, Antonio Tassino, had associates in many of the key positions in the state. Ludovico managed to sidestep attempts to remove him again by moving the young Duke Gian into a castle under his control. With Gian now in his uncle's hands, Ludovico became regent of the state.

The young Gian was married off in 1489 and his marriage was soon fruitful. But each child that Gian fathered threatened to move Ludovico further from his growing hopes of ruling Milan in his own name. However, Ludovico needed to make more allies if he was to become duke. He also needed to remove any remaining rivals, and he employed various tactics to do so. In one instance, Filippo Eustachi, one of the most powerful men in the state, was tricked out of his castle, accused of treachery with the Holy Roman Emperor and imprisoned for life.

One of the most momentous events in Ludovico's life was not one of his attempts to seize control by force but his marriage in 1491 to Beatrice d'Este, one of the most eligible women in Italy. Normally a marriage of such importance would be consummated immediately but Ludovico apparently chose to wait for a month until his fifteen-year-old bride was willing to sleep with him. Her family was furious, since without a consummation the marriage could be annulled. However, they need not have feared as Beatrice soon held Ludovico in her sway.

UNKNOWN NICKNAME

To history, Ludovico Sforza is known as 'Il Moro' – The Moor. It was a name attached to him from childhood but unfortunately no one bothered to record why. Some have said it was because Ludovico had a dark complexion; others that it derived from the word for mulberry, a fruit he cultivated (both the head of a black man and a mulberry were symbols Ludovico employed in art commissioned for him). However, most historians think Il Moro is simply a childish play on Ludovico's middle name of Maurus.

In 1494, Gian suddenly died. The rumour was spread that he had succumbed from having too much sex with his wife, but others thought that it was more likely Ludovico poisoned the young duke. Ludovico was certainly pleased when the Milanese nobles offered him the ducal crown instead of passing it to any of Gian's children.

If Ludovico ruled Milan, then Beatrice ruled him. All observers of the time remark on her beauty and vivacious personality, and it seems certain that Ludovico was captivated by her. Money was lavished on entertaining Beatrice and her pleasure was his only pleasure. When Beatrice gave birth to a son, the line of Ludovico seemed assured. She became one of Ludovico's most important assets as she skilfully managed diplomatic campaigns and charmed King Charles VIII of France.

Ludovico nearly crumbled when Italy erupted in war between a group known as the Holy League and the French. He planned to abandon his city out of fear but only Beatrice's insistence on fighting on kept him in the war. Ludovico seems to have suffered a stroke and Beatrice stepped into his role. She was made the governor of Milan and personally rallied the armies to stop a French invasion. Wherever Ludovico was, his wife was seen supporting him and managing affairs of state.

Once peace was assured in 1495, Ludovico might have expected to enjoy a long reign with his impressive spouse securing their position. However, when Beatrice died in childbirth in 1497, Ludovico collapsed in grief. His hair is said to have turned white and he spent weeks in darkened rooms, refusing to see anyone. A special room for mourning, painted entirely black, was created for his extravagant melancholy. Every possible marker of honour was created for Beatrice, including coins struck with her image and grand monuments.

In 1499, the armies of France once again marched on Milan. Without Beatrice by his side, Ludovico put up little resistance. He fled the city but was eventually captured by the French and held captive for the rest of his life. Ludovico is said to have become mad after his loss and, after attempting to escape in 1508, he was placed in a dungeon where he soon died.

IVAN THE TERRIBLE

When people picture Ivan the Terrible, the first Tsar of Russia, their image is probably drawn from the nineteenth-century painting by Ilya Repin. In this artwork, Ivan is shown as an old man, eyes open wide in maddened horror, clinging to the body of his dead son. But this is not a painting of a man mourning the loss of a beloved child, it actually shows the moment after Ivan has brutally beaten his son to death. Terrible indeed.

The man who would become known as 'the Terrible' was born in 1530 as the oldest son of Vasili III, Grand Prince of

Moscow and all Russia. While much of Europe was glorying in the artistic and social revolution of the Renaissance, Russia held firmly to its traditional ways of life. Vasili III died, painfully, of blood poisoning when Ivan was just three years old and although Ivan was hailed as the new grand prince, his government was not immediately settled. Vasili's brothers Yury and Andrey might have fancied their chances as regents, but Ivan's mother Elena took control of the state. Within a few years, both Yury and Andrey had been arrested and died in prison – an early lesson for Ivan in how to deal with threats to power. Elena herself died in 1538 from suspected poisoning and Ivan fell into the hands of competing *boyars,* powerful nobles.

Ivan, as Grand Prince, was only useful to the nobles when he was needed to oversee ceremonies to lend legitimacy, otherwise he was kept in stark conditions and mistreated by his regents. Ivan later wrote of the rags he was dressed in as a boy. There were rumours that the young ruler found an outlet for his impotence by attacking animals since he could not strike at the boyars – at least not yet. When he was thirteen, Ivan made his first move at taking control of his life and nation. At a feast, he suddenly rose and accused one of the most powerful boyars, Prince Andrei, of ruining the state and called for him to be arrested. The hapless Andrei had not expected his ward to act against him and must have looked confused as he was hauled away to prison and execution. Reports that he was torn apart by dogs are probably a later invention.

In 1547, Ivan was anointed as the first Tsar of all Russia during a sumptuous coronation. Tsar, derived from Caesar, was a title which showed Ivan was laying claim to the legacy of ancient Rome and proclaiming Russia (and its ruler) as one of the great powers of the world. Ivan was also declaring that God had chosen him to rule, meaning that to challenge him was an act close to heresy. To go with his new title, Ivan needed to forge a new and more centralized state which would never allow the boyars to mistreat him again.

There were a flurry of changes, such as the creation of a national assembly to help the government and a council of nobles to advise the tsar, as well as reforms to the way in which the hinterlands of Russia were managed. To shore up his leadership, Ivan also created the country's first standing armies. The zeal for fairly innocuous modernization came to a crashing halt in 1553 when Ivan fell seriously ill. He called on his nobles to swear an oath of loyalty to his infant son and heir, but when the boyars saw how close to death the tsar was, many of them refused the oath, thinking another prince might serve them better. Many who said improvident things at this moment of crisis would not live long enough to regret them, for when Ivan recovered he did not forgive the intransigent boyars. Ivan's cousin Vladimir, a potential rival to the throne, is said to have refused to kiss a crucifix to mark his obedience to Ivan's son. This refusal turned out to be a deadly blunder; Ivan said grimly that whatever happened next was on Vladimir's soul, not his.

UNLUCKY IN LOVE

Ivan's heir was born to his first wife, Anastasia, who was known for restraining some of his worst impulses. But when she died in 1560, he suspected poisoning and blamed the boyars for her murder. His next wife also died young, some suspecting Ivan himself of her poisoning. Ivan's next wife lasted less than a month before dying, which sparked a wave of executions when Ivan suspected yet another poisoning. His fourth wife failed to give him a child after two years and so she was sent to a convent as a nun, a fate suffered by his fifth wife, too. Ivan's sixth wife managed to give birth to a son and also had the luck to outlive him.

It is often said that Ivan's personality changed completely following his illness but there was evidence of his tendency towards violence earlier when he led armies against his enemies. It is recorded that he personally beat one enemy to death. Folktales said that Ivan carried a staff with a vicious spike on the bottom. To test his boyars he would stab their feet while talking to them to see if they would speak out.

Once recovered and having carried out reprisals against some of the boyars who had shown disloyalty, Ivan still felt that many nobles were against him. In 1564, he left Moscow and undertook a pilgrimage to a fortified monastery. Somewhat unusually, he had taken the entire royal treasury with him on pilgrimage, which should have been a warning to those left behind. Ivan announced his abdication, accusing the nobles of treachery and the clergy of impiety. Fearing the hostile countries surrounding Russia and potential chaos within the state, the boyars begged Ivan to retake the throne – which he did only after they agreed to grant him a vast tract of land under his sole control. He was also allowed to create a bodyguard known as the *oprichniki*, who would become his private army and the first secret police in Russia. The *oprichniki* carried out swift and bloody retaliations against Ivan's perceived enemies. Many nobles were executed. Ivan's cousin Vladimir had his home burned down, faced internal exile, and was later arrested and killed along with his family.

Vladimir had lands near Novgorod, which was in an area vulnerable to attack by Lithuania and Sweden, Ivan's enemies in the long-running conflict known as the Livonian War. Ivan feared that Novgorod would defect, as the town of Izborsk had done in 1569, and he suspected both the nobility and common people of treachery. Ivan at this time was constantly perceiving plots against himself, and dozens of boyars had been executed.

Ivan advanced on Novgorod with both regular troops and his secret police, executing anyone who was even considered a possible traitor. En route to the city, more than 30,000 people were slain and the clergy were tortured into handing over their riches. In the middle of a frozen January in 1570, the horrors of Ivan's army arrived at the gates of Novgorod.

The *oprichniki* were unleashed. In the attack on Novgorod, people were executed by being pushed under the frozen ice of the river, burned to death or simply beheaded. Everything of value was taken and homes were pulled down. When it was found that starving poor people were eating the dead, the cannibals were executed. The massacre went on for weeks.

In 1581, the tsar and his oldest son, also called Ivan, fell into a quarrel about the tsar's brutal treatment of his daughter-in-law. In a moment of rage, Ivan the Terrible struck his heir on the head with his staff. The younger Ivan fell to the ground dead. This murder meant that the throne would pass to Ivan's only other surviving son, Fyodor, a wildly unsuitable tsar due to his mental and personal troubles. Ivan the Terrible died in 1584, and in the wake of his son's weak leadership, Russia fell into a period known as the Time of Troubles.

AURANGZEB

The legacies of tyrants can cause powerful emotions long after the tyrant has died. In 2025, uproar was caused in the legislative assembly of Maharashtra state in India after a member praised a Mughal emperor who had died in 1707. Other members accused the speaker of treason and he was later suspended. The question of whether the tomb of this emperor should be removed has led to violence and death. Even to mention the name of Aurangzeb is to court controversy between Muslims and Hindus.

The Mughal Empire was founded by Babur in the early sixteenth century when he invaded India from the north. Babur was a Muslim who set himself up as the ruler over a Hindu population, so from this earliest point there was tension between the religion of the ruler and that of the ruled. Accounts of Babur's conquests in India refer again and again to the 'infidels' he faced, but a later emperor, Akbar, introduced a policy of 'universal peace' with the aim of smoothing tensions between all religions in his realm.

This peaceful coexistence was not always successful under his successors. Wars against Hindu states were occasionally framed as *jihad*s (holy struggles) and Hindu temples were sometimes pulled down. Yet at other times, the Islamic Mughal emperors also sponsored the construction of Hindu temples. The record of Mughal relations with Hindus can still stir up passionate controversy today and no emperor is more discussed than Aurangzeb.

The Mughal court was not one which was always filled with familial loyalty. Inheritance of the throne did not necessarily go to the oldest son, and so princes of the blood sometimes had to bloody their hands if they wished to grasp the sceptre. Aurangzeb was born as the grandson of the Emperor Jahangir in 1618 and was soon embroiled in family infighting. Aurangzeb's father Shah Jahan rebelled against Jahangir and

Aurangzeb was handed over as a hostage for his father's future good behaviour. His captivity did not last long as Jahangir died the next year and Shah Jahan emerged as the next emperor, swiftly executing any royals who might have had a rival claim.

The lives of princes are well documented and so we know that Aurangzeb was a clever child whose main interests were literary, though focusing on the study and learning of the Quran. He was not only a bookish boy, however. When an elephant rampaged towards the royal family after a staged elephant fight, Aurangzeb, aged just fifteen, rode towards it and hurled a spear at its head. Aurangzeb was knocked from his horse, but for his bravery his father awarded him his weight in gold. Aurangzeb did not hesitate to compare his actions with the supposed cowardice of his brothers, who he insinuated (perhaps falsely) had held back from confronting the beast. It never hurts to plant the seeds of your eventual success early in life.

Aurangzeb was given plenty of opportunities to show his military prowess when he was appointed to govern rebellious regions of the empire. During his first campaign as nominal commander of an army, he took the opportunity of tearing down a Hindu temple and erecting a mosque on its site. Aurangzeb was often set tasks of great difficulty in harsh conditions which led to stalemates or eventual failure, but he learned the ways of war. Despite his service, it seemed that his father was grooming Aurangzeb's brother Dara to take charge of the empire after his own death, and, indeed, when Shah Jahan fell ill, Dara was made regent. In 1658, the four sons of Shah Jahan started a war to see who would be the next emperor.

BURIAL OF A LIFETIME

Aurangzeb's mother was Mumtaz Mahal, the most beloved wife of his father. When she died in 1631, the emperor ordered the construction of a vast funeral complex of pure white marble complete with a domed tomb. Its construction cost would equal billions of pounds today. Known as the Taj Mahal, it has become one of the most famous buildings in the world.

Aurangzeb triumphed after a series of battles which saw all of his brothers fleeing into exile. Dara was captured and handed over to Aurangzeb's mercy. He was thrown onto an elephant besmirched with filth and paraded through the streets to the jeers of the people. Aurangzeb charged Dara with heresy, and Dara was soon put to death. Although Shah Jahan survived his illness, Aurangzeb did not allow him to recover the throne. He was deposed and held in confinement, allowed to view the Taj Mahal through a window.

Under Aurangzeb, the religious tolerance which had marked Mughal rule was heavily curtailed. He applied a tax known as the *jizya* which was levied in many Muslim states and paid by

all non-Muslim inhabitants. This tax had been abolished by earlier emperors but Aurangzeb sent out Muslim tax collectors to gather it, which prompted a rebellion by the Hindus of north India. The celebration of Hindu festivals was also severely restricted in some areas. Another of his acts which angered his Hindu subjects was desecrating a temple by slaughtering a cow in it. Also, when Sikhs protested against forced conversions to Islam, he had their leader Guru Tegh Bahadur beheaded.

Aurangzeb proved his own commitment to Islam by learning the Quran by heart after he ascended the throne. He also stopped presenting himself daily on a palace balcony for the adulation of his subjects, as other emperors had, since he felt it was too close to being worshipped. In Lahore, he ordered the construction of what would be the largest mosque of its time.

While Aurangzeb is routinely described as demonic by Hindu sources, historians are divided about whether he was really as doctrinaire and repressive in his religious policy as many believe. Many of his actions seem to have been prompted by political circumstances, but, whatever the causes, they led to widespread outrage at the time. Throughout his reign, the Mughal armies were almost constantly called on to march out and put down revolts. Even Aurangzeb's own son Akbar joined a revolt against him.

Despite these setbacks, Aurangzeb was able to extend the Mughal empire in the course of his rule. He introduced reforms to the judicial and legal systems which centralized power ever more in his hands. Yet this caused unrest among the groups who were denied their traditional privileges. The economy grew to become the largest in the world at the time, but through constant war and the lavishness of his court, the treasury was nearly emptied.

Aurangzeb died at the age of eighty-eight in 1707. Even in his final days, he held to his conservative Islamic faith. When courtiers suggested he give an offering of an elephant and rich jewels for his recovery from illness, he dismissed it as a ridiculous practice. Aurangzeb was buried in a simple tomb, unlike that of his mother, with only the sky above it. Following his death, the Mughal empire began its slide towards collapse.

With his divisive legacy, Aurangzeb is thought by some to be one of the worst tyrants in history, while others consider him to have been a strong and pious man. Effigies of Aurangzeb were burned in the streets in 2025, a level of feeling accorded to few historical figures.

CATHERINE THE GREAT

Sophia Augusta Frederica von Anhalt-Zerbst-Dornburg faced a number of serious stumbling blocks on her path to the throne of Russia. For a start, she had only the most tangential connection to the Russian imperial family and absolutely no claim to the crown. Next, she was born in 1729 in Prussia, part of the Holy Roman Empire. Lastly, she was a woman,

which has historically been a bad idea if you want to exert your authority. So how did she become not only leader of Russia, but earn the epithet 'the Great'?

Catherine (as she was later called) was born into a minor princely family. Her mother, Joanna, had been raised by her godmother at one of the most lavish courts in Europe but on her marriage found herself living in relatively humble surroundings. This fall from luxury seems to have driven her to dream of making spectacular matches for her children which would return the family to wealth. Catherine found her mother to be cold and occasionally violent.

Joanna had two pieces of luck in her plans for greatness. Her brother Adolf Frederick had become the guardian of an orphaned relative, a boy called Karl Peter Ulrich – who just happened to be the only living grandson of the Russian Tsar Peter the Great. Joanna took Catherine to meet him and though the young girl was immediately repulsed by Karl Peter, at the time that was no bar to marriage.

The other stroke of luck was that, in 1741, Empress Elizabeth ascended to the throne of Russia. She had been betrothed to another of Joanna's brothers, Charles Augustus, who had died before the marriage took place, and Elizabeth still treasured his memory. When Elizabeth took Karl Peter as her heir, it also made Joanna's brother Adolf Frederick the heir to the Swedish throne and so raised Joanna's family in prominence. Joanna struck at once and sent a message to Elizabeth to reignite their friendship. In 1744, Joanna was commanded to bring Catherine to the Russian court with an eye to Karl and Catherine becoming engaged, which they duly were. Catherine became wife to the heir to one of the richest thrones in Europe.

It might have seemed like a fairy tale except Peter, as Karl Peter had become, proved to be a disappointing prince and a worse husband. He was childish and had to be told not to tell rude jokes in public or pull grotesque faces at banquets. Catherine would later recount stories of Peter playing with toy soldiers in his bedroom. When a rat once destroyed one of his toys, Peter had the culprit caught and hanged. He also failed to win over his people, while Catherine was assiduous in showing her devotion to the Orthodox faith and Russian traditions. Despite Peter's drawbacks as a husband, he and Catherine managed to produce a son – although most of her younger children were not Peter's, as Catherine had sexual relationships with a number of attractive men during her marriage.

When Peter III took the throne following Elizabeth's death in 1762, he managed to succeed in upsetting most of those who might have supported him. He withdrew Russian forces from the Seven Years' War and gave up most of the advantages they had won. Next he planned to use the Russian army in a war against Denmark to protect the duchy he had inherited in Germany. It would have no benefits for Russia and would have cost them dearly. His plans for social change also drew criticism by stripping power from nobles and claiming church lands. Catherine was plotting a more extreme change within months of her husband's rise to the throne. One of Peter's last mistakes was to humiliate Catherine at a public banquet, reducing her to tears. Opinion in important circles shifted towards Catherine and her son.

In June 1762, Catherine mounted a horse, rode to the guards' barracks in St Petersburg and was proclaimed to be the ruler of all Russia. Peter III, away from the city, did not even notice that he had been deposed even as his wife was blessed by a bishop and invested with imperial power. Commoners, politicians, nobles, soldiers and sailors all swore allegiance to their new leader. Peter III's resolve to fight for his throne collapsed almost at once and Catherine, wearing the uniform of a soldier, travelled to arrest him. Peter was confined and soon after died, officially of an attack of haemorrhoids, but many suspected the former tsar was quietly disposed of. In her memoirs, Catherine claimed that all she had done was 'to save myself, my children, and perhaps the empire also, from the wreck of all the moral and physical qualities of this Prince.'

Having usurped her husband's throne, Catherine was crowned in an extraordinary ceremony when the Grand Imperial Crown, constructed for her, was placed on her head. Adorned with nearly 5,000 diamonds, it was a sign of the glory Catherine hoped for her reign. Catherine was clear that she was no mere regent for her son and heir; she was the reigning empress.

Perhaps most remarkably for a woman who had no claim to the throne she now possessed, Catherine proved a shrewd and successful empress. One of her main aims was to bring Russia more in line with the European powers in terms of economy, education and military strength. Economic reforms were necessary because of the many wars Russia engaged in over the course of her reign. As a result of these, Russia managed to take large areas of Ukraine from the Ottoman Empire and gained access to the Black Sea.

Many of Catherine's favourites profited from her patronage. Stanisław Antoni Poniatowski, the son of a Polish count, with whom Catherine had a two-year affair, was raised to the throne of Poland when it became vacant in 1763. Yet again a man let Catherine down, as he did not prove to be the puppet she hoped for and she had to quash his attempts at reform. When a rebellion broke out against him, Russia and Prussia simply stepped in and divided the country between them. Catherine may have ruled as modernizing autocrat but she was still an absolute monarch.

Catherine had to be careful not to make the same mistakes which lost Peter III his throne. There was discontent with some of her actions and when this happened there were outbreaks of revolt. Sometimes these rebellions brought out pretenders who claimed to be her dead husband. All were put down. One of the main risks to Catherine's rule came from her son Paul. He was, after all, the son of the last tsar and so had the legitimate claim to the throne. She simply kept Paul at a safe distance from the court.

Catherine the Great died in 1796 after a rule of thirty-four years. One of her son's first acts established that the throne would always pass to the eldest son of the tsar. Paul I's greatest fear was another Catherine the Great.

EQUINE DEATH

One of the most famous tales about Catherine the Great is that she met her end being crushed to death under a horse with which she was trying to have sex. It was said that the horse slipped from a special harness which had been constructed for the act. Catherine, who was no stranger to human lovers, would have recognized this as just another of the scandalous rumours which dogged her throughout her reign.

MAXIMILIEN ROBESPIERRE

Looking for heroes in history is a tricky pastime. You might find someone who on the surface appears to be ahead of his time: forward-thinking on matters of democracy, an eighteenth-century lawyer deeply opposed to the slave trade, and the person who coined the slogan 'Liberty, Equality, Brotherhood'. Surely such a one could never be accused of tyranny – he advocated the death of tyrants. And yet blind adoration of Robespierre, a man who expressed all these views, led to some of the darkest times in the French Revolution.

Maximilien-François-Marie-Isidore de Robespierre, as his vaguely aristocratic name suggests, was born into a prosperous family in 1758 in France. At this time, Louis XV was king of one of the most absolute monarchies in Europe. His court at Versailles consumed much of the annual revenue of France as nobles vied with each other to live extravagantly inside what was both a centre of government and a gilded cage. All of this was paid for with taxes taken from the common man, as nobles and clergy were exempted from many forms of taxation. Yet there were thinkers in France at this time advocating for a change to the system.

Robespierre proved to be a brilliant child and received a fine education at some of the most prestigious institutions of the day to study law. He was appointed to be a judge in 1782 but, according to his sister's later account, he faced huge moral doubts about his right to sentence another human to death. She described him pacing around the house, unable to eat for days, even though he knew the guilty party was a murderer. Perhaps he was most offended by the brutality of executions at the time, when the guilty were horribly tortured before being hanged. Robespierre wrote around this time that executions should be swift and painless decapitations.

By 1789, France was drowning in debt due to its expenditure in support of the rebellious British colonies in North America. Spending money in order to weaken Britain was easy, but because of the archaic financial system employed by the French state it was far harder to gather money. King Louis XVI, a weak and vacillating monarch who had ascended to the throne in 1774, was forced to call a meeting of the Estates General – the assembly representing commons, clergy and nobles – to look for ways to remedy the situation. Robespierre was elected as one of the representatives and, like many, he wanted more than financial change.

While the cost of grain was spiking and people went hungry, the representatives arriving at Versailles could not help but notice the opulence of court life. Robespierre had already questioned the legitimacy of the Estates General since the nobility cared only for the nobility, the clergy were selected by the church, and most common people had no time to consider political matters as they spent all their time trying to scrape together enough food for their families. He was already talking of the 'enemies of the state' who were undermining the majority.

Unfortunately for Louis, calling together a group of clever and ambitious men with grievances backfired. When the nobles and clergy united to block any change which might result in them having to pay any more tax, the commons withdrew and formed their own National Assembly with the aim of creating a new constitution for France. This was the beginning of the French Revolution and Robespierre was in it from the start.

With the fall of the Bastille prison, symbol of the French crown's absolute power, and when a crowd marching on Versailles dragged Louis and his family to Paris, it seemed that the revolutionaries were unstoppable. Yet no one was certain what form the revolution would take and factions coalesced around the differing conceptions of a new France. Robespierre joined the Jacobin Club, one of the more radical groups of the revolution.

The revolution found many supporters in the cities, and revolutionaries like Robespierre viewed themselves as champions of the people, whether the people appreciated it or not. In fact, many French people were suspicious about attempts to remove power from the king, who had been traditionally seen as the protector of the people and appointed by God. King Louis XVI was forced to go along with many of the developments pushed by the revolutionaries, but he never truly believed in any of their changes to the constitution.

In 1791, the king and his family made a failed attempt to flee from France and engage foreign aid to quash the revolution. When he was captured and brought back, it was clear that the revolution and the monarchy could not coexist. Robespierre delivered a blistering attack on Louis for his perfidy and the Jacobins leapt to their feet and gave an oath to defend Robespierre's life.

Louis was deposed and placed on trial in front of the National Convention in 1792. When he was found guilty of treason, Robespierre was the first person to vote for the king's immediate execution. Louis was transported to the Place de la Révolution (now the Place de la Concorde) and his head was unceremoniously severed from his body by the guillotine.

KINDLY EXECUTIONS

The guillotine with its swiftly falling blade was designed as a humane method of putting people to death. It was also a democratic method of murder as everyone, regardless of rank, was killed in the same way. It became a symbol of the revolution and women could be seen sporting earrings in the shape of the guillotine.

With the king gone and a republic set up, Robespierre acted swiftly to protect the new state of affairs from enemies both foreign and domestic. Wherever he looked, there were those he saw as enemies of the people. Robespierre called for the Jacobin Club to fight against those who were opposing their view of the revolution. Slowly but surely, Robespierre identified himself with the revolution and any attack on him became seen as an attack on the revolution.

His enemies began to die. Georges Danton, Camille Desmoulins, and other leading lights of the French Revolution who had taken differing opinions to Robespierre, were dragged to meet their fates at the guillotine. During this period from September 1793 to Robespierre's death in July 1794, known as the Reign of Terror, more than 10,000 people were executed and many others died without ever reaching trial. Robespierre lamented that he was being blamed by everyone for this and was now viewed as a bloody-handed tyrant. Eventually, even the most ardent revolutionaries tired of the constant falling of the guillotine's blade, and it was decided the year of terror had to end. As the man in charge of this, Robespierre had to be removed.

In 1794, Robespierre entered the National Convention to be faced with a wave of denunciations. When he, who had spoken so eloquently in favour of revolution, rose to speak in his own defence he was shouted down. Robespierre was so outraged he struggled to get any words out and his enemies said it was the blood of his victims that was choking him. Robespierre left and an arrest warrant for conspiracy against the Convention was issued.

When guards arrived to capture him, Robespierre turned a gun on himself. Instead of ending his life, all he managed to do was blast his jaw to pieces. In agony, he was led through a screaming mob and mounted the scaffold to the guillotine. To ensure his neck was bare, the fabric holding the shattered jaw in place was ripped away, and on 27 July Robespierre died screaming in the same place as so many of the people he had sentenced to death.

NAPOLEON

It is naive in the extreme to think that a progressive leader cannot also be an autocratic dictator. No one better encapsulates the ethos of the Enlightened Despot than Napoleon Bonaparte, who conquered much of Europe and set about reforming the legal code of the lands he ruled while also crowning himself as a new emperor. Napoleon's career was built on the bodies of his enemies, and more than a few of his own men.

Napoleon entered the world at just the right time to make the most of his talents. When he was born in 1769 on Corsica, it was just one year after the island had been placed under the power of France and so he was a French citizen. It was lucky that Napoleon's godfather was the new French governor of Corsica, giving him a powerful supporter. At a young age, he was sent to a military academy in France but, under the royalist regime, where advancement was mostly based on nobility of birth, he would otherwise have had no prospects of a decent career given his provincial origins.

Following the French Revolution, with its rallying cry of equality for all, Napoleon could now look forward to a vertiginous rise through the ranks – if only given the opportunity to show his skill in war. Since Napoleon had learned the tactics of modern artillery, he soon came to the attention of the revolutionary leaders, who were at war with many of their neighbours as well as internal rebels. When royalists attempted an uprising in 1795, the government placed its defence in the hands of Napoleon. He was heavily outnumbered, but through tactical emplacement of cannon he was able to drive off the rebels with what he called 'a whiff of grapeshot'.

His brilliant and deadly actions earned him the favour of the government and he was rewarded with the command of an army sent to invade Italy. You would need a thick book to chart Napoleon's military path but suffice it to say he beat every army sent against him and led a march towards Vienna, which so threatened the Austrians that they made peace with France. He also showed a magpie's tendency to send artistic and archaeological treasures back to France as trophies of his victories. Napoleon became famous and increasingly powerful. As he remarked when called to return to France from Italy, 'I have tasted command, and I cannot give it up'.

PRIZES OF WAR

Italy provided many treasures which Napoleon used to dazzle the people at home. From Venice, he plundered the Horses of St Mark, bronze sculptures created by the ancient Romans and already stolen from Constantinople by the Venetians in 1204. So many marble statues were taken from other cities that they arrived in a pile in Paris and were haphazardly stored in kitchens and hallways until places could be found for them.

Perhaps hoping to equal the triumphs of Alexander the Great, Napoleon set out to conquer Egypt for the French. As well as being a spectacular victory it would offer the French a route to India. Napoleon took with him a huge team of scholars to collect the treasures of antiquity, including the Rosetta Stone which unlocked the secrets of hieroglyphics. Unfortunately for Napoleon, after the Battle of the Nile in 1798 many of his trophies were captured by the British and shipped to London. In 1799, Napoleon found governing his Egyptian conquest was not going well and so returned to France – leaving his army behind to deal with the mess. But Napoleon was not fleeing from disaster, he was running towards victory.

The government in Paris, known as the Directory, was in a shambles. The wars were not going well and the treasury was nearly entirely depleted. Public opinion was turning against them. It was not turning against Napoleon, however, as he had mastered the art of publicizing his victories. As a strong man who seemed to offer security to France, he became the central figure in a plot to overthrow the government. When Napoleon spread a false rumour that there was to be rebellion against the government, the leaders decided to give Napoleon complete control of all troops nearby. He then used these to arrest the members of the Directory and carry out a coup. In the aftermath, Napoleon and two others were designated consuls in control of the state. Napoleon was able to rid himself of his two companions and declared himself First Consul for life in 1802. A plebiscite ratified this appointment with 99.7 per cent of respondents approving of it – at least according to the figures Napoleon released.

Despite this unimaginable level of public support, there were still republicans who did not want to see one man hold all the power, while royalists wanted a different man to hold all the power. Plots to remove Napoleon were swiftly put down but created an excuse for Napoleon's next promotion. The best way to forestall more conspiracies was to create a position that could not be questioned. In 1804, Napoleon summoned the pope to crown him as emperor. At the final moment, Napoleon took the crown from the aged pontiff's hands and placed it on his own head.

Alongside a self-aggrandizing upgrade to his title, Napoleon wanted to reform the French state according to his own ideas. New educational academies were created which removed teaching from the hands of the Catholic church and presented opportunities for the brightest to rise in society. His greatest achievement, however, was a new legal system known as the Napoleonic Code. The laws of the old regime were swept away and replaced with the best Enlightenment thinking of its day with a focus on civil rights held by citizens, even if the rights of women were still subject to their male relatives.

In battle, it seemed as if Napoleon was unstoppable. Again and again, he beat back coalitions of nations ranged against him. The British offered vast sums of money to countries willing to fight Napoleon, yet he seemed to triumph every time. His relatives found themselves being placed on thrones across Europe. Napoleon's brother was made king of Spain and his son the king of Rome. But no person can be lucky forever, and when you have triumphed as often as Napoleon, the temptation to hubris is almost irresistible. The need to field large armies, and replace soldiers lost in campaigns, began to bleed France dry of young men.

When Russia defied Napoleon by evading his command not to trade with Britain, he assembled the largest army he ever fielded and invaded Russia in 1812. Some 600,000 men marched in this Grande Armée. Although Napoleon managed to capture Moscow, the Russians refused to offer terms. Napoleon was cut off from supplies in a ruined city. The magic of his genius failed him and he refused to see how perilous his position was. When forced to retreat through a harsh Russian winter, Napoleon fled ahead of his army, leaving hundreds of thousands of his own men dead behind him.

Then, by late 1813, Lord Wellington was invading France from the south and Britain's allies were attacking in the north. With Paris under threat and insufficient men to fight all of his enemies, Napoleon faced reality and abdicated his throne. It might have been kinder to kill the one-time emperor but instead the victors exiled Napoleon to the small Mediterranean isle of Elba. A man for whom domination of Europe had not been enough would never settle for this, however. In 1815, Napoleon returned to mainland France and began the Hundred Days of his attempt to recapture his empire.

Troops flocked to him and Napoleon positioned himself as the man to liberate France from the foreign forces occupying it. However, after defeat at the Battle of Waterloo, no one in France believed Napoleon could bring France anything other than more war. He was taken to the lonely island of St Helena in the South Atlantic for his final exile under British guard. For the rest of his life, Napoleon's empire went no further than the garden of his small house. He died in 1821, his death perhaps hastened by the arsenic pigment in his wallpaper.

RANAVALONA I

. . . .

The Kingdom of Imerina (or Madagascar) was founded in 1540, before the age of European colonization across Africa and Asia, however it could not escape the encroachment of Europeans forever. In the nineteenth century, a female ruler emerged who pursued policies aimed at limiting their influence on her land – but with extreme costs to her people.

Princess Ramavo was born into the royal house of the kingdom but not in direct line to the throne. Her rise came when her father helped reveal a plot against the then-king, and as a reward Ramavo was married to the king's heir, Prince Radama. Radama became King of Madagascar aged seventeen in 1810, and set about securing his reign – by murdering rivals, including some of his wife's family, and by suppressing rebellious subjects. He also sought relations with European powers to modernize his army and bring technology and literacy to his society.

These moves at Westernization were not universally popular. New military technology allowed Radama to bring more of Madagascar under his control, but many people were wary of the Christian missionary schools he permitted in his kingdom. When Radama died of alcoholism in 1828, he had no son, so by rights the throne should have passed to a nephew. However, other plans wert in motion.

Various factions, particularly those who rejected European interference, manoeuvred Princess Ramavo onto the throne as Ranavalona I, the first ruling queen of the kingdom. Ranavalona followed tradition in putting her husband's sisters and their sons to death to secure her new crown. In time, many in Madagascar would come to call her rule 'The Dark Years', and the British Press referred to her as the 'Mad Monarch of Madagascar'. In 1829, Ranavalona bore a son, also named Radama, who was, in line with tradition, considered to be the king's son – though eleven months had elapsed between the first Radama's death and the birth of the second.

The probable father of Ranavalona's son was a young military officer called Andriamihaja, who had supported her usurpation of the monarchy. The queen's lover became her first prime minister, but he had powerful enemies at court and was suspect because of his conversion to Christianity. In 1831, he was accused of treason and executed.

With her coronation supported by the most conservative elements in the kingdom, Ranavalona was emboldened to undo much of the work her husband had set in motion. Trade deals with France and Britain were torn up and the actions of missionaries tightly monitored. When the French sent a naval expedition against Madagascar in 1829, the royal army was able to fend them off and capture several French soldiers who were beheaded. The French temporarily retreated but found malaria to be just as deadly an enemy as Ranavalona, and abandoned the attack in the face of ever greater losses.

Lack of trade with Western powers stopped the supply of modern weaponry to her army but fortune supplied an alternative. While attempting to recover sunken treasure near Madagascar, a French engineer named Jean Laborde found himself also shipwrecked, was rescued and was brought before the queen. His knowledge of weapon manufacturing allowed Ranavalona to create her own industry to arm her soldiers.

To build a strong kingdom that could withstand both internal and external pressures, Ranavalona relied on traditional practices. Madagascar was a highly stratified society and the lower ranks owed service to those above them in a form of unpaid labour known as *fanompoana*. Once, it had been considered an honour to undertake this forced labour when called upon, but Ranavalona used coerced workers to make up for shortfalls in manpower created by the large army she developed. Laborde was placed in charge of thousands of unpaid workers to build his manufacturing plants, as well as palaces for the queen.

Queen Ranavalona was also known to enjoy alcohol and while under the influence of drink she could be convinced to execute members of the court as traitors. She also relied on the traditional ordeal by tangena nuts to identify who was plotting against her. The tangena nut contains several deadly toxins and so shavings of the nut were fed to suspects as a way of ascertaining their guilt.

NUT TRIALS

Suspects were fed three pieces of chicken skin and then parts of the poisonous tangena nut. The body would attempt to expel the poison and so the suspect's vomit was examined. If the victim vomited up all three bits of chicken, they were innocent, otherwise they were carried off for execution. Even those who vomited everything up might have already absorbed a lethal dose of toxin, and those who died despite vomiting were judged to be guilty. It is thought that under Ranavalona around 3,000 people per year died in tangena trials, and the majority of her subjects would have experienced it at some point in their lives.

Ranavalona, though she had been friendly with Christian missionaries, began a harsh suppression of Christians in the 1830s. Christian rites were banned and Christians themselves faced death and persecution. According to (probably embellished) accounts published in England, and lapped up by a Christian audience, the persecuted were executed by being stabbed by spears, skinned alive, burned alive or killed by having boiling water poured over them.

As well as preserving traditional forms of governance, Ranavalona was responsible for creating a modern bureaucracy to help run her kingdom. She was also successful in warding off foreign intervention. In 1845, a law was passed which brought any foreigner in Madagascar under her authority and imposed on them the duty of performing forced labour. Most Europeans left. A joint British and French force attacked the port of Tamatave as a punitive measure, but was rebuffed.

Ranavalona's whims could prove deadly. In 1845, she decreed that there would be a grand procession through her realm in which the whole court and their slaves would take part. Unfortunately, there were no roads good enough for this journey and so thousands were set to work constructing them at an incredible rate in advance of the royal party. The queen did not provide sustenance for her thousands of attendants and workers, and perhaps 10,000 people died of starvation.

Europeans did not give up trying to infiltrate Madagascar. Several plots were hatched to depose Ranavalona, including with the connivance of her own son. The European powers recognized that they would have a better chance of doing business under his rule. These schemes were detected and the plotters captured. One of them was the ever helpful Laborde, who escaped execution and was simply exiled. Ranavalona was never defeated by her enemies. She died in 1861, aged around eighty-two, and her son inherited the throne and began the process of opening Madagascar to the world.

Ranavalona I is a complex figure. She was undoubtedly effective in protecting her country from European powers that were gobbling up lands across the globe. The traditions of her people were championed and preserved. She also kick-started a form of modernization. It cannot be overstated, however, just how destructive her rule was for the nation she saved from colonization. Estimates vary but it is thought that during her reign the population of Madagascar fell from around 5 million to around 2.5 million.

WILLIAM WALKER

In the middle of the nineteenth century, the United States was torn between those who believed in the right to own slaves and those who opposed slavery. Attempts were made to limit the areas where slave-holding was permitted but for rich southerners who wanted to exploit more land with slavery there were always other options: if only they could conquer new lands, they could work their slaves there. Enter one William Walker, who attempted to carve out a domain of his own by force in Latin America. Such unauthorized military campaigns were known as filibustering – and Walker made several incursions into sovereign states as a filibuster. A secret society named the Knights of the Golden Circle dreamed of creating a slave empire based in Cuba and made up of much of Mexico and northern South America.

William Walker was born in 1824 in Tennessee and trained as both a doctor and a lawyer, but did not find these professions to his taste. In 1849, he became a journalist in San Francisco. Walker proved to be rather bellicose and fought a number of duels against those who slighted him. Unfortunately, he was not a crack shot and, in his final duel in 1851, he was hit in the thigh.

After recovering from his wound, Walker committed himself to annexing parts of Mexico. The idea of Manifest Destiny – that the United States would spread across all of North America – was common at the time, and Walker wanted to make sure that he would control a chunk of it. Despite having no military training, he managed to convince around fifty men to join him in an attack on the Baja California peninsula of Mexico. In 1853, this ragtag army captured the town of La Paz and seized the Mexican governor. Walker declared the formation of the Republic of Lower California, with himself as president.

It was easy to issue a Declaration of Independence and give followers government positions but it was not easy to hold on to this new nation. Walker had written against expanding slavery but, perhaps realizing support could come from southern slavers, he used a law code which allowed slavery in his republic. The only support he received came from rogue adventurers out to make money and find excitement, but they proved so unruly that some of them had to be whipped and shot. No help came from the United States government.

When the Mexican government sent forces against him, Walker found he had to undertake a slow retreat to the United States with his dwindling army. The Republic of Lower California lasted only a few months. Walker was put on trial for waging an illegal war in violation of the Neutrality Act. It would be hard to argue against the evidence in favour of conviction, but a jury took less than ten minutes to declare him innocent.

Walker's experience did not put him off filibustering and another opportunity presented itself in 1854. Nicaragua was a small country in a strategically important place. Since the gold rush in the American West, a swift way of sending ships from the east to the west coasts was highly desired. If a canal could be cut across central America then it would be a boon for commerce. Many in the United States might be interested in such a project. A civil war in Nicaragua provided the perfect chance to take control.

Walker was invited to settle a colony in Nicaragua by the president of the country in hopes of support against his rivals. Walker arrived with sixty soldiers of fortune in 1855 and joined the fight. There were setbacks for Walker's men but they managed to defeat the rebels a number of times and forced both sides to come to terms.

TEACHER'S DAY

Each year on 29 June, Teachers' Day is celebrated in Nicaragua. The national celebration of teachers stems from the heroic actions of schoolteacher Enmanuel Mongalo y Rubio against Walker's forces. During the Battle of Rivas, he ran with a flaming torch into the house where Walker's men were hiding and burned the building to the ground.

A provisional government of Nicaragua was formed under President Patricio Rivas, but with Walker as the head of the army there was no doubt who was really ruling the country. Not everyone in Nicaragua was pleased with this turn of events and the minister of war was found to be in secret contact with Honduras. He was tried for treason and executed: Walker would not tolerate any threat to his new domain. To curry support with adventurers and investors from the southern states of the United States, Walker decided to reintroduce slavery to Nicaragua after it had earlier been abolished.

There were signs that the government in Washington would recognize the Walker regime, but Nicaragua's neighbours had no desire to have mercenary conquerors on their borders. In 1856, Walker did away with any pretence by declaring himself president of Nicaragua after an election where he ran unopposed. Costa Rica, Honduras, El Salvador and Guatemala then formed an alliance to drive Walker out. Walker's forces were ground down and, in 1857, he was forced to surrender. Instead of facing justice on the spot, Walker left for the United States on a navy boat and was welcomed as a military hero. He left thousands dead in his wake. As just one example, Costa Rica had played the major part in defeating Walker's army, but its soldiers returned from the war bringing a cholera epidemic that killed 10 per cent of Costa Rica's population.

Not to be discouraged by defeat, Walker attempted to launch another attack on Nicaragua just six months later but was arrested before he could set out. Foiled again, he looked elsewhere for a kingdom. In 1860, British colonists on Roatán island in the Caribbean invited Walker to join them as they were afraid of being annexed by Honduras. Walker took a hundred men and captured the Honduran port of Trujillo.

This was to be Walker's last exploit. He found himself trapped between Honduran forces and British naval vessels. Walker surrendered to the Royal Navy but the British, perhaps not wanting Walker disturbing the peace in the region any longer, handed him over to Honduran officials. Walker was executed, and his dreams of his own land died with him. All that was left to him was a piece of ground six feet long.

FRANCISCO SOLANO LÓPEZ

Everyone wants to help their children succeed in life. When you are a dictator, it must seem like the natural next step is to groom a child to take over as supreme leader once you are gone. The results of this nepotism have rarely been more disastrous for a nation than in the case of Francisco Solano López, dictator of Paraguay from 1862 to 1870.

López was the son of Carlos Antonio López, first president of Paraguay. The older López was an elected leader, but was given increasingly long terms in office and the right to decide who would follow him. As a dictator, the father was rather more lenient than most, and managed to create a thriving economy as well as abolishing slavery. Carlos López had gained international recognition for his country under the slogan 'Independence or death!' The choice between these two ideas would be made for Paraguay under the rule of his son.

Francisco Solano López was left an improved army by his father and had been placed in a position to use it. He had, after all, been named a brigadier general of the Paraguayan armed forces at the age of just eighteen. To be fair to the López leadership, Paraguay was an embattled nation as it was surrounded by neighbours who either wanted to take their territory away or change the government. To guard the nation he would inherit, López studied fortification technologies assiduously both at home and abroad. During the Crimean War, he had travelled with the French army and seen how strong locations could be besieged.

LADY MACBETH OF PARAGUAY

It was while in Paris in 1854 that López met an Irish courtesan called Eliza Lynch. While the pair never married, they would have a lifelong relationship, and Lynch would in time become the First Lady in the state. During the war that shaped López's leadership, Lynch constantly accompanied him on campaign. At the time, many of the blunders of the war and her lover's ambition were blamed on Lynch.

During the later years of his father's rule, López became minister of war and then vice president. Carlos Antonio López died in 1862 and his son moved swiftly to assume the presidency. He was confirmed in the position for ten years, but would not enjoy the full term.

At first, López had everything going for him. He was personally popular, looked fine in a uniform, spoke the language of the common man and could enjoy the support of a press system that acted as a propaganda wing of the government. Anyone who spoke out against the leadership would find their words being reported to the authorities. Given his genuine abilities and his complete control of Paraguay, López must have felt untouchable, but he would soon test himself against the geopolitical realities of his day.

López had inherited a nation that was focused on survival and improving its economy, but he wanted to place Paraguay among the leaders of South America. Argentina and Brazil were the major powers of the region and López did not want to always be at their mercy. The boundary lines of these nations had been contested since their independence from their European masters, and both countries frequently intervened in the affairs of their less powerful neighbours. López decided Paraguay could offer protection to the smaller South American nations.

An alliance was formed between Paraguay and Uruguay, and López tried to prepare his army for battle. Unfortunately, with Paraguay being a landlocked nation, due to a blockade the modern weaponry he bought from Europe would never arrive. When Brazil looked to invade Uruguay, López issued a letter stating that any attack on Uruguay would be taken as an attack on Paraguay. Brazil invaded Uruguay in 1864 and López declared war. He would also declare war on Argentina. His faith in the army he had developed apparently bordered on hubris, for Brazil alone could call on manpower and resources many times greater than Paraguay's.

Uruguay was overrun and its government replaced with one favourable to Brazil's interests. López had already sent his army against Brazil, though, and the war would not go away.

In 1865, the Treaty of the Triple Alliance was signed between Brazil, Argentina and Uruguay with the express aim of driving out the government of López as a threat to the security and stability of the region. With seemingly the whole world united against him (and by extension his nation), López resolved to fight until the bitter end. It would be bitter indeed.

The fighting in the war which followed centred on the rivers as these were the main pathways of transportation in the region. The terrain was undeveloped and conditions were difficult. The Brazilian navy was able to block the rivers and so Paraguay was largely cut off from receiving material aid from the outside world. The Paraguayan army found itself fighting a modern war with antiquated guns for which they could not always get ammunition.

Paraguayan forces were pushed back into their own country and the war turned into a grinding defensive action. López was constantly on the move to rally his nation, but morale is no substitute for soldiers. War in the nineteenth century was less against human enemies and more against illness. Wherever armies camped, the unsanitary conditions would breed epidemics. Thousands of Paraguayans died.

As the war dragged on into 1868, López found himself questioning those around him. In his mind, conspiracies and plots were being formed to topple him. When a tyrant is afraid, people tend to end up dead. In this case, hundreds of citizens holding important positions were rounded up, summarily tried and executed for their perceived treachery. Even his brother was taken for questioning and López is said to have whipped his own mother when she revealed he was born out of wedlock. López lost the battle which followed this massacre of Paraguayans, so the purge did not even secure his position. The shine was beginning to come off his legend. He was drinking increasing amounts and gaining weight from a fondness for cakes while his soldiers were starving.

In 1869, the armies of the allied nations stormed into the Paraguayan capital, forcing López to flee into the wilderness with a handful of men. By the next year, López was surrounded and, along with his meagre force, decided to fight to the death rather than surrender. He was injured and captured but continued to spit defiance at the foe, shouting, 'I will die with my country!' He did just that moments later.

Had López's war only led to his own death then it might be easy to look on it as a magnificent stand for one's nation. Unfortunately, Paraguay ended the war with perhaps half of its population having been killed by fighting, famine or disease. The vast majority of adult men in the country were dead or had fled. Paraguay was then occupied and portions of its land seized by Brazil and Argentina.

The legacy of Francisco Solano López is hotly contested. For some, he is a national hero who stood up for his country against bullying neighbours, and he is still celebrated by many in Paraguay. For others, he was the ruin of his nation. For many of his countrymen, he was death.

IV

Modern History

Empress Dowager Cixi

In the treacherous and cut-throat environment of the Chinese imperial court, no one rises to the peak of power by accident. One has to place oneself in the right situations to be noticed, identify those who could harm you, outmanoeuvre rivals and often drive them into exile or death. A woman who successfully managed these schemes and effectively ruled over China for nearly fifty years was Empress Dowager Cixi. She was born into a low-ranking noble family in 1835 and became one of the lowest rank of concubines selected for Emperor Wenzong (the Xianfeng Emperor) of the Qing dynasty. She entered the Forbidden City, the imperial complex in China's capital Beijing, aged seventeen.

Wenzong had inherited the imperial throne in 1850, but instead of anticipating future glories, he must have wondered whether he would live to enjoy his reign. China was in crisis in the nineteenth century due to natural disasters, governmental failures and foreign interventions revealing the relative lack of power of the emperor. The First Opium War in 1839 had seen the British Empire use military force to strong-arm the Chinese into allowing the lucrative import of opium into China to continue. Things worsened following Wenzong's rise to power. The Taiping Rebellion broke out late in 1850 and would spiral into one of the bloodiest revolts in world history. The Chinese state was soon rocked by other insurrections and difficulties. It was into this pressured world that Cixi stepped.

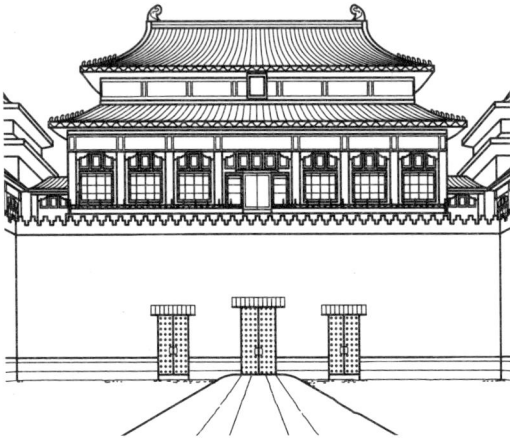

YOUNGER BROTHER OF CHRIST

The Taiping Rebellion was led by Hong Xiuquan, a man driven to a breakdown by his repeated failures to pass the imperial examinations to enter the civil service. While mentally unbalanced, he experienced visions in which it was revealed to him that the Christian God the Father was in fact his own real father, and Jesus was his elder brother. Thousands flocked to Hong Xiuquan and his teachings about how China had been led astray. When the authorities attempted to disperse the crowd, Hong's followers fought off the imperial forces and the Taiping Rebellion began.

We know little about her life in the imperial court early in Wenzong's reign but Cixi must have seen the pressure on the emperor. When the Taiping rebels captured the city of Nanjing, the emperor wept publicly. The treasury was so depleted at this point that the emperor was forced to sell off imperial treasures to raise funds and his concubines were ordered to give up most of their jewellery. Cixi was a woman with a mind, and she attempted to use it by offering unsolicited advice to the emperor on how to deal with the problems besetting China. This was a blunder, as the emperor turned on this woman who dared interfere with his rule. However, Empress Ci'an, the emperor's primary wife, was able to protect Cixi. Then, in 1856,

Cixi gave birth to the emperor's first (and only surviving) son and she was raised in rank to just below the empress.

Cixi's position allowed her to place some of her family members in positions of power, and by their marriages, she strengthened her ties to the imperial family. In 1860, the Chinese state was humiliated during the Second Opium War when British forces sacked and destroyed the Old Summer Palace, one of the most splendid wonders of China. Emperor Wenzong and his courtiers were forced to flee Beijing, and in 1861, he died aged just thirty. Cixi's five-year-old son became Emperor Tongzhi and she was raised to the status of empress dowager. Wenzong had named eight officials to rule as regents for his young son, but these were soon displaced by Cixi.

Cixi formed an alliance with Empress Dowager Ci'an to divide power between themselves and rule through Tongzhi. Together with Wenzong's brother Prince Gong, they led a coup when Cixi blamed the regents for the shame of the loss in the Second Opium War. In an act of clemency, Cixi only ordered the execution of three of the regents, and that by simple beheading instead of having them slowly sliced to death – a long-standing Chinese method of execution. Of the two ruling women, Cixi was the more astute political figure and she began to directly advise ministers. She knew how to project power – instantly changing from jokes and smiles in privacy to intimidating glares when in public. Slowly, she manoeuvred herself into becoming the only true power in China, even managing to sideline Prince Gong.

Cixi began a series of reforms determined to stabilize the state which she now controlled. The complex bureaucracy that governed China was overhauled – with several executions of officials to encourage others to curb bribery and inefficiency. To develop better relationships with European powers, she also created the first Chinese office of foreign relations. Education was opened up to teachings from the West in an attempt to modernize China.

As Emperor Tongzhi reached manhood, Cixi was forced to look for a consort for her son. Unfortunately, the one chosen clashed with Cixi and the emperor began to show more attention to her than to his mother. Cixi instructed that the two should be kept apart. This did not lead to a stable young monarch and he started to mistreat his staff and lost himself in the pleasure houses of the capital. When Tongzhi came of age and was given complete charge of the state, he, predictably, proved a disaster. In 1874, he tried to strip power from all of Cixi's allies, prompting her to appear at court and publicly rebuke him. Conveniently for Cixi, Tongzhi died suddenly the next year.

Cixi then selected her four-year-old nephew to succeed to the throne as Emperor Guangxu. In 1881, the Empress Dowager Ci'an, Cixi's only rival for authority, also died suddenly and many suspected Cixi of poisoning her. Because of her long period in charge of the government, most officials felt a great deal of loyalty for Cixi, and she was able to retire from direct control in 1889 as Emperor Guangxu came of age, without loss of much authority. In retirement she lived in great luxury, even employing maids to light and hold her pipe while she smoked. But she also received copies of governmental memos and used her influence to decide policy matters.

Emperor Guangxu saw that China, and his place on the throne, were dependent on modernization. He launched the Hundred Days' Reform in 1898 which included creating a constitutional monarchy, building trade schools and abolishing the long-standing examinations for would-be imperial officials. All these reforms were laudable, but were too much too fast for conservatives who believed in the supremacy of traditional Chinese culture. Cixi sensed that such changes might destabilize the throne she had worked so hard to buttress, and so she led another coup to drive Guangxu out of power by confining him inside the palace. Six of Guangxu's advisors were beheaded. Cixi then simply ruled in Guangxu's stead.

In 1900, the Boxer Rebellion broke out with rebels seeking to eradicate foreign influences in China. Cixi saw these rebels as a useful tool to strengthen China's independence, even at the risk of antagonizing the European powers. The Boxer Rebellion did indeed provoke Western intervention and an eight-nation alliance invaded China and battled their way into Beijing, where Western diplomats and traders were under siege.

Cixi was forced to flee her capital. Her advisors counselled her to carry on a war against the alliance, but she was more clear-sighted and accepted the peace terms that were offered, even though they were humiliating and expensive.

Back in the capital, Cixi sponsored reforms that were more moderate than those which had led to the downfall of Guangxu. By 1908, she was beginning to sicken and knew that death would come for her soon. Emperor Guangxu was also stubbornly clinging to life after years in captivity. If Cixi died before him, she feared that he might restart what she thought were his disastrously extreme policies. He died on 14 November, and tests on his body have shown he had massive amounts of arsenic in his system. After writing Guangxu's will, Cixi swiftly announced the elevation of his nephew, a two-year-old boy called Puyi, as the next emperor. After this final act of control, Cixi died on 15 November.

LEOPOLD II OF THE BELGIANS

At its heart, an empire is simply a machine for extracting wealth and resources from lands that are not your own, and all too often the wheels of these machines have been greased with the blood of colonized peoples. Any monarch who presided over an empire can be considered a tyrant to those they ruled over, but the most naked example of imperial tyranny belongs to King Leopold II of the Belgians.

The nation of Belgium was formed following the 1830 rebellion of the southern portion of the Netherlands. To gain legitimacy it was decided that a king was needed, and so Prince Leopold of Saxe-Coburg-Saalfeld was chosen to become King Leopold I as a constitutional monarch of the Belgian people. His power was hemmed in by the constitution and the new Belgium had no overseas territory in the way Britain or Spain did. Leopold I's son, who became Leopold II, found this a most unsatisfactory state of affairs.

Almost as soon as Leopold II came to the throne in 1865, he started to cast about for potential sites to colonize. He was convinced that the only way for Belgium to become a real country was to build an empire with himself at the head, but unfortunately other European countries had gobbled up most of the rest of the world. Leopold II tried to buy the Philippines from Spain and looked everywhere from Brazil to Haiti and Hawaii for potential colonies. However, there was one major difference from the colonization efforts of other nations: Leopold II had no intention of handing new lands over to his democratic government, he intended to hold them as personal property.

In the nineteenth century, there were still areas on European maps of Africa that were blank. This gave the impression that they were uninhabited and ripe for exploitation, which may have surprised the millions of Africans who lived there. Readers of European newspapers were thrilled with dispatches from darkest Africa which recounted the exploits of daring explorers. Pious Christians funded missionaries to bring the light of Jesus to the native peoples.

IN SEARCH OF LIVINGSTONE

David Livingstone was a missionary and explorer of Africa who thought commerce and Christianity would stop the slave trade in Africa. He disappeared for six years and so a New York newspaper sent Henry Morton Stanley to find him. In 1871, Stanley found him beside Lake Tanganyika and greeted him with the famous phrase 'Dr Livingstone, I presume?'

Leopold II recognized that Africa offered the best opportunity for him to build his empire. If he could explore the Congo River basin in central Africa and construct stations to conduct trade, he could extract the natural wealth of the area. In 1876, Leopold hosted the Brussels Geographic Conference at which famous explorers and philanthropists agreed to form the International Association for the Exploration and Civilization of Central Africa, giving Leopold's plans for the Congo a humanitarian gloss. Leopold set up many such organizations to cloak his true activities in Africa.

Leopold sent the explorer Henry Morton Stanley to explore the Congo to help understand what was there. At the same time, Stanley sought out local leaders and convinced them to sign treaties which essentially handed their lands and the labour of their people to Leopold for nominal fees, such as a few pieces of cloth. Thanks to Leopold's cunning, he managed to convince other European nations to recognize what he called the Congo Free State as a legitimate entity, under the control of one of his organizations, but really under the personal ownership of Leopold himself.

At first the main export of the Congo was ivory, which Europeans used for everything from billiard balls to piano keys. The difficulty was getting the ivory out, as much of the Congo river was filled with rapids and so boats could not operate along its full length. Leopold ordered the construction of a railway to bypass the rapids – but building a railway in hard terrain cost the lives of thousands of workers, most of them Africans. Leopold was never afraid to sacrifice others' lives for his plans.

With the discovery that rubber made excellent tyres, the major export of the Congo Free State became natural rubber. This had to be gathered by hand in an intensive and backbreaking process. Leopold decided that any land that was not being directly cultivated was now the property of the state and he sold the rights to exploit it to various companies, most of which developed rubber plantations. European adventurers flocked to work as overseers in the Free State with the offer of high wages and absolute freedom to govern their workers as they saw fit. The Congolese were forced to work the rubber plantations and given huge quotas that they had to fulfil.

The Congolese were little more than slaves and their treatment was entirely at the discretion of their overseers. Conditions were uniformly brutal. To enforce cooperation, the *Force Publique*, an army of Africans under the control of European officers, was created. When they considered a worker to have been lazy, one of the most common punishments they dished out was a thrashing with a whip made from hippopotamus hide.

If an entire community was judged to be uncooperative, then the Force Publique might burn down all their homes. Hostages were taken. The soldiers were not allowed to use their guns for private hunting, so for every bullet fired they had to prove it was for legitimate purposes of killing rebellious Congolese. Their proof, presented to their superiors, was a severed hand of their victim. There were reports of hands being cut from the living as a punishment, sometimes from children to encourage their parents to work harder. All of these murders left many orphans, but the Force Publique swept them into orphanages where they were raised to be the next generation of Force Publique soldiers.

It is impossible here to fully explore the horrors of the Congo Free State. It is also impossible to calculate how many people died under this regime from either directs acts of violence, overwork or waves of epidemics. Modern estimates suggest that the population of the state fell by up to 50 per cent – around 10 million people. There was an uncountable number of cases of mutilation, torture and rape.

For Leopold II, the sheer inhumanity of his regime seems not to have mattered. Money flowed out of the colony and directly into his pockets. With this money he funded churches, museums and palaces in Belgium. He was so active that he became known as the Builder King. But the good times for Leopold could not last.

In 1900, a French-British part-time journalist, Edmund Dene Morel, was working for a shipping company that traded with the Congo and noticed that, despite the mountains of ivory and rubber being shipped to Europe, all that the Belgians ever sent back were guns, bullets and shackles. No one was paying for the goods Belgium received, meaning that they must have been produced by slave labour. Morel started a campaign to publicize the atrocities of the Congo Free State. Many people provided him with information and investigators were sent to the Congo to report on conditions there. The horrors of Leopold's tyranny had become public.

In 1908, the uproar was so great and so embarrassing for the Belgian government that they forced Leopold to give up the Congo Free State. Don't worry too much for Leopold – he was compensated for his loss with millions of francs. Before handing over the colony, Leopold ordered the destruction of all records to conceal all that had happened, so the cruelty of his empire will never be fully known. Leopold died quietly in 1909.

JOSEF STALIN

In 1956 a crowd gathered in Stalin Square in Budapest and milled around the 8-metre-tall statue of Josef Stalin which symbolized his domination over Hungary. With blowtorches, cables and tractors the statue was toppled and dismantled by people longing to be free of Soviet Russian control. The revolution in Hungary was swiftly crushed under the tracks

of Soviet tanks, but ironically many of the statues of Stalin in the Soviet Union were removed in a process known as de-Stalinization following his death in 1953.

The man who would become Josef Stalin was born in Georgia in 1878 with the name Ioseb Besarionis dze Jughashvili. He was a bright boy but suffered early in life at the hands of his alcoholic father and an accident which left him with a damaged arm. Ioseb entered a seminary to become an Orthodox priest and did well at first. But God did not hold his interest for long. Soon the lessons of Marxism and communism dominated his mind.

Ioseb gathered workers to discuss labour conditions and began organizing demonstrations and strikes. His role as an agitator was noticed by the Russian authorities who sent him into exile in Siberia in 1903. Ioseb managed to escape but later actions suggest that he recognized the potential of sending enemies to Siberia. Once out, he allied himself to the Bolshevik Marxists who called for direct action to overthrow the corrupt government. Ioseb proved to have a talent for inspiring violence in others, and around 1912 he adopted the name Stalin, derived from the word for 'steel'.

By 1917, World War I had gone very badly for the Russian Empire. The tsar was deeply unpopular for his failure to lead Russia to victory and people were fed up with the constant shortages caused by the wartime economy. The tsar abdicated and middle-class politicians set up a new democratic system – but failed to address many of the issues driving public discontent.

In those unsettled times, Stalin was highly active in pushing forward Bolshevik agitation. When he took charge of the safety of the Bolshevik leader Vladimir Lenin and hid him from the authorities, Stalin was left as the foremost party member. After the Bolshevik revolution, Stalin became one of the commanders in charge of fighting off counter-revolutionaries.

Following Lenin's death in 1924, Stalin was conspicuous in his mourning and associated himself in any way possible with the revered former communist leader. Through wily manoeuvres and playing factions against each other, Stalin was able to drive his main rival, Leon Trotsky, from Russia and, by 1929, held total control of the state.

ICE AXE AND ASSASSINS

Trotsky survived longer than many of Stalin's enemies – and more than a few of his supporters – would. In 1940, Trotsky was living in Mexico and well used to dodging assassins sent by the Soviet secret services. An agent called Ramón Mercader managed to infiltrate Trotsky's circle and was left alone with the older man. He struck Trotsky's skull with an ice axe, delivering a fatal blow. Mercader was arrested and imprisoned for his crime, but following his release in 1960, he was awarded the Order of Lenin and the title Hero of the Soviet Union.

Stalin had no desire to rule over a backward nation. He wanted to contend with the Western powers and he wanted to do it quickly. To modernize the USSR, he set high, sometimes unreasonably high, targets for the outputs of agriculture, mining and industry. To increase food production, he ordered collectivization of farms, blaming failures in agriculture on relatively prosperous peasant farmers called *kulaks*. Land was pooled, harvests seized and political agents dispatched to ensure the policy was followed. In the Ukrainian famine that resulted from this doctrinaire action, millions starved to death.

Stalin enforced socialist policies, even when reality did not conform to his ideas. For example, the controversial scientist Trofim Lysenko created a theory of biology with socialist analogies and so he was placed in charge of Soviet genetic research. When this theory failed, people starved, but scientists who refused to adopt it were imprisoned. Anyone who dared fail to meet Stalin's demands faced being dragged away by the Soviet secret police in the middle of the night. Thousands were executed for treason, while many more were sent to gulags to work in horrific conditions which often proved to be as effective a death sentence as a bullet in the brain.

The prisons and graveyards of the USSR were filled during Stalin's Great Purge of the late 1930s. The nation was purified of any potential source of dissent. Many of those who had served with Stalin in the early days of the revolution now found themselves under suspicion. Scientists, writers and other intellectuals were arrested or shot. History itself was purged when photos were doctored to remove images of people who had since been arrested.

Of course, Stalin did not carry out his murders himself. In Lavrentiy Beria, he found the perfect tool. The head of the secret police from 1938 to 1946, Beria was sadistic in his brutal torture and executions. Stalin never lost his trust in Beria.

Though Stalin knew the threat of the German Nazi regime, with their hatred of communism, he still chose to ally himself with them in 1939 with the aim of carving up Poland between them. Once in control of portions of Poland, the Soviets murdered over 20,000 Poles in the Katyn Massacres to remove potential threats.

It came as something of a surprise to Stalin when the Nazis broke the non-aggression pact and invaded Russia in 1941. The German advance was swift and savage, leaving Soviet defences in tatters and the army, which had been purged of experienced leadership, seemed powerless. Nazi bombs were soon falling on Moscow itself. Stalin would not allow the country to lose to Germany, no matter how much blood needed to be expended to win. Orders were issued stating that those who surrendered would be considered to be traitors. Wave after wave of Soviet troops were sent into battle.

Soviet industry had to be rebuilt further to the east to replace the tanks and planes destroyed in the early months of the war. Tough enforcement saw production soar and soon the Soviets, with Western aid, were able to start pushing the Nazis back. When the end of the war came into sight, Stalin began to make territorial demands to his allies, which included Soviet control of eastern Europe.

Almost immediately after World War II ended, a Cold War began between Western democracies and the Soviets. The 2 million captured Soviet soldiers who returned to Russia were investigated to ensure they did not bring back any anti-Soviet tendencies. Stalin had dragged his country through one of the most destructive wars in human history and he did not intend to lose the peace.

Stalin's final years were still filled with paranoia. When treason was suspected among the mainly Jewish doctors at the Kremlin, he had them rounded up, tortured and executed. This left few doctors willing to treat Stalin's failing health for fear of what might happen to them. When Stalin had a stroke alone in his room in 1953, his staff were scared to check on him and left him on the floor for hours, lying in his own filth. Once he was discovered, attempts were made to treat him, but it was too late. Stalin died days later. He was entombed with full honours beside Lenin.

The Soviet leadership had to contend with Stalin's legacy, both the cult of personality and his crimes. In 1956, Nikita Khrushchev denounced the terrors of Stalin's rule to the Politburo and began the process of freeing the Soviet Union from the worst excesses of Stalinism. The statues of Stalin began to fall soon afterwards.

While the statues of Stalin were quietly mothballed as the cult of Stalin was disassembled, his shadow looms large over Russian history. He may have done terrible things but he was also credited with victory over the Nazis in the Great Patriotic War, as World War II is known in Russia. A cruel but strong man still holds appeal to many Russians. In 2025, a sculpted monument of Stalin surrounded by adoring citizens was unveiled in a Moscow subway station.

BENITO MUSSOLINI

Fascism was given its first expression on the world stage in the 1920s by Benito Mussolini, when he took charge of Italy with dreams of forging a new Roman Empire. Other dictators

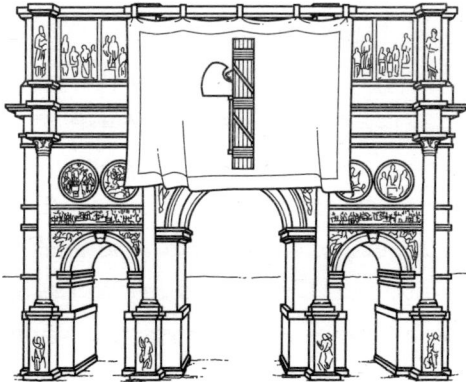

would learn from his example how useful fascism could be in conquering first their own nation and then turning their military loose on others.

Mussolini was born in 1883 to a family with strong socialist beliefs and for many years he followed these left-wing views. As a boy, he often showed a taste for violence but he managed to achieve good scores at school and was regarded as a promising child. He qualified as a schoolteacher, and learning under him must have been a nerve-wracking experience. Mussolini found his pupils 'quite meek', though almost everyone would be shy around Mussolini.

Mussolini travelled to Switzerland to avoid serving in the Italian army but soon returned and became one of Italy's best known socialists. He wrote journalism, essays on social matters and even a novel attacking priests, as well as editing one of the major socialist newspapers. When Italy went to war with Libya in 1911, he took part in demonstrations and denounced the war as an imperialist action.

When World War I broke out, most socialists wanted Italy to remain neutral but Mussolini loudly proclaimed his support for going to war. He was cast out of the Socialist Party. This was a key moment in the creation of fascism as Mussolini came to preach nationalism as the driving force of social advancement. Conscripted into the Italian army, he served on the front lines and was invalided out in 1917 after an accident.

Coming out of the war, Italy was denied many of the territorial claims it had pressed for, even though it had been on the winning side. The governments of Italy were notoriously unstable and prime ministers could rise and fall in as little as sixteen days; few lasted more than a couple of years. Mussolini felt that the Italian people, whose nation was often pushed aside by more powerful countries, would be attracted by ideas of stability and strength. So he formed the Fascist Italian Combat Squad and published a fascist manifesto.

The manifesto called for many things that strike us as reasonable, such as universal suffrage and a minimum wage. It spoke to a population suffering from economic stagnation. But the fascists also believed in creating 'living space' for Italians by taking back former Roman possessions around the Mediterranean. Mussolini claimed that there was a hierarchy of peoples, and with Italians supposedly at the top it was only right that they should conquer lesser races and their land.

Mussolini used the unsettled state of Italian politics to push fascism forwards. He won popularity among soldiers now left unemployed and crying out for a strong man to direct them. His supporters, known as Blackshirts, were not averse to using thuggery to beat up socialists and communists. A common punishment for those who stood against the fascists was to be bound to a chair, beaten and force-fed the laxative castor oil. The policies of the fascists were also fluid enough to take advantage of any opportunity to win votes and support

MOTHER OF FASCISM

Mussolini was not a faithful husband and one of his most prominent mistresses was Margherita Sarfatti, a Jewish art critic. Though she started as a socialist, she became one of the best-known propagandists for the fascist movement. Unfortunately for Sarfatti, when the Italian fascists enforced anti-Semitic policies in the late 1930s, she was driven out of the country by the very government she had helped create.

wherever they could. Mussolini was elected to the Italian parliament in 1921.

In 1922, Mussolini organized a March on Rome with tens of thousands of Blackshirts descending on the capital to demand the ousting of the prime minister, Luigi Facta. By this point, the fascists were already acting as the true rulers in many areas, and, fearing a civil war, King Victor Emmanuel III refused to back Facta, who resigned. Control of the government was passed to Mussolini as the new prime minister.

As he had few representatives in the elected chamber, Mussolini needed to solidify his support, which he did by changing the law to suit his needs. Having then gained a majority in parliament, his path to dictator, under the title *Il Duce* ('The Leader'), was set. Mussolini's glowering bulldog face appeared everywhere and, as a former journalist, he knew how to pull the levers of public opinion. He took credit for interventions that worked, such as making trains run on time – even when they didn't. When persuasion failed, he could always rely on the application of violence, or the threat of it, to get his way.

In 1935, Mussolini ordered his armed forces to invade Abyssinia. The League of Nations proposed economic sanctions but Italy simply withdrew from the League and carried on the war. The Italians used the best modern weaponry to inflict the worst harm on Ethiopians, including through the use of mustard gas. Hundreds of thousands died as a result of the invasion. During the Spanish Civil War, tens of thousands of Italians fought on the side of the nationalists, committing further crimes.

The rise of Hitler in Germany was not necessarily good for Mussolini. German territorial aims in Austria clashed with Italian aims. But in 1939, Italy and Germany entered a military alliance known as the Pact of Steel. Mussolini had gambled on a quick victory for his German friends and hoped to feast on the spoils. It was a bet he would come to regret; the Italian military was in no way prepared for a total war.

Mussolini's forces invaded Egypt from Libya but a vastly outnumbered British force was able to push them back and take over 100,000 Italians prisoner. When Mussolini invaded Greece, it was a disaster for the Italians. Italian weapons manufacturing was a shambles and soldiers could not be sure their bullets would fire as intended. The Germans were forced to intervene on behalf of their Italian allies, diverting troops that they really needed elsewhere.

With the war turning against the Axis powers and Allied bombs falling on Rome itself, in 1943 Mussolini's government allies turned on him. The Italian king was emboldened to dismiss Mussolini. Although Mussolini had been cheered into office, there was no outcry from the people when he was marched from power and placed in 'protective custody'. Italy pulled out of the Axis and declared war on Germany – but the Nazis merely took control of the north of Italy. The Germans sent a raiding party to free Mussolini from his imprisonment and abducted him to be their puppet in the north.

In 1945, Mussolini realized the era of fascism was ending as the Allies fought their way up the Italian peninsula. He tried to flee to Switzerland but was captured by communists, and Mussolini and his mistress were arrested and shot. The corpses of Mussolini and several other fascist leaders were exposed in a public square in Milan, hung by their ankles for the crowd to jeer at.

ADOLF HITLER

No tyrant has been more studied, written about and dominated the popular imagination quite like Adolf Hitler. As the driving force of the Nazi regime of Germany, his rule led to world war

A TASTE FOR WAR

Hitler's hatred of the multi-ethnic Austro–Hungarian empire saw him move to Munich in 1913 to avoid serving in its army. That is how he found himself in a crowd there on 2 August 1914, the day after Germany had declared war. A photograph of the scene happened to capture Hitler in the throng, cheering at the prospect of fighting. The image was taken by Heinrich Hoffmann, who would later become Hitler's personal photographer. Hitler soon volunteered to join the Bavarian army to get his first taste of combat.

and genocide on a scale that is almost unimaginable. It takes books far thicker than this one to document even a fraction of the horrors he unleashed and the pain he inflicted. Hitler was just one man, though – how did he convince others to carry out his demented policies or persuade them to look the other way as millions died?

Adolf Hitler was born in 1889 in Austria, part of the Austro–Hungarian Empire, just across the border from Germany. People who examine his childhood for the causes of his tyranny point to Hitler's violent father, loss of a brother to illness, and inability to follow the rules in school. In his youth, Hitler began to idolize Germany for its strength, and despise the dissolute Habsburg monarchs of Austria–Hungary. After the death of his father in 1903, Hitler was free to explore painting, which was his first love.

After moving to Vienna, his pedestrian and old-fashioned watercolours failed to impress in a world where art was tending toward bright new ideas. Hitler was twice rejected by the academy of arts and he was forced to make a living doing whatever odd jobs he could find. Vienna had a large Jewish community at this time and to a floundering Hitler this flourishing group was an easy target to blame for his failings. The Austro–Hungarian empire included many Slavs, and Hitler also learned to hate them.

World War I was the making of Hitler. He never rose higher than private, but enjoyed the camaraderie of his fellow soldiers, and won some of Germany's highest military honours for his bravery. He was injured several times, allowing him to claim he had bled for Germany. After Germany surrendered in 1918, he would always argue, despite all evidence to the contrary, that Germany had been winning the war before it was 'stabbed in the back' by Jews and traitors.

Hitler began working as a military intelligence officer to gather information on the right-wing parties springing up across the defeated Germany. As part of this work, he joined the nationalist and anti-Semitic Germany Workers' Party and impressed its leaders with his public-speaking skills. When he left the army, he devoted himself to this organization, which had renamed itself the National Socialist German Workers' Party – or Nazi Party.

Hitler led his first coup when he seized the leadership of the Nazis in 1921. The German economy was in a shambles, with huge war reparations to be paid, and people were crying out for someone to blame. Hitler served up fiery speeches explaining why many Germans were penniless – he particularly blamed Jews and communists. People flocked to hear how they were not responsible for their troubles.

In 1923, Hitler led an attempt to take over the whole of Germany. His plan was to first seize the Bavarian government and use pressure to drive out the unstable national government in Berlin. This 'Beer Hall Putsch' was a flop, and easily crushed by police. Hitler was sent to prison, but national coverage of his defence gave him fame and won him more adherents. He used the time in prison to write *Mein Kampf*, his book that explained exactly what he planned and whom he would later target. It was fantastically successful, therefore making the Nazis' aims clear to everyone: they would acquire more land for Germany, and would rule over the people and 'races' they thought were inferior. With Germany so weak, many chose to ignore the warning signs and follow only Hitler's promise of renewed strength for the country.

When things got worse for Germany in the Great Depression, support for the Nazi Party only got stronger. Poverty is a powerful driver for extremist beliefs. Hitler also won over wealthy industrialists who feared socialism more than fascism. In 1933, the Nazis gained the largest share of the vote in the election and Hitler became chancellor of Germany. Partly through intimidation, Hitler was given the right to make laws without needing the approval of parliament, and he quickly banned all other political parties. Concentration camps started to fill with trade unionists and members of opposition parties. After the death of President Hindenburg in 1934, Hitler declared himself the sole *Führer* (Leader) of the German Reich. Now, not only fanatical Nazis were supporting his aims, but everyone who simply did their government jobs was indirectly propping up Hitler.

Hitler set about re-arming the nation in defiance of treaties meant to limit Germany's military capabilities. He also enacted laws targeting Jewish citizens. Propaganda relentlessly described the Jewish population as a disease which had to be eradicated. In 1933, Jewish people were banned from government employment, then they were slowly removed from all economic life of the country before finally being stripped of their citizenship and made second-class Germans. Nazi paramilitary groups ruthlessly attacked Jewish individuals and organizations.

The Nazis created a cult of personality around Hitler which framed him as the only man able to rescue Germany, and many Germans began to believe it. He had a number of successes on the world stage, such as unifying Germany and Austria and seizing part of Czechoslovakia, which gave credence to the notion of Hitler as a man of destiny. Hitler himself believed this myth – with disastrous results.

World War II broke out in 1939 and at first Hitler's strengthened armed forces seemed unstoppable as they rolled over Europe. His promise of providing Germans with 'living space' in eastern Europe seemed to be coming true. However, he would, of course, first have to remove the people already living there. In 1942, Hitler approved plans for the Holocaust, which aimed to kill anyone he viewed as less than human. Jewish people, homosexuals, communists and many others were now sent to death camps for immediate slaughter or were worked to death in inhumane conditions to supply equipment for Germany. Six million Jews and millions of others were systematically murdered by the Nazis.

As well as the death camps, Hitler's regime saw many other atrocities, such as barbaric medical experiments, the execution of prisoners of war and the slaughter of whole villages in reprisal for attacks against German invaders. Overall, at least 30 million – possibly as many as 60 million – people died in the war.

Hitler would not accept that any of his plans could be wrong; after all they had worked so well early in the war. As problems began to mount, he ignored the advice of others. The Nazi invasion of the Soviet Union ground into a bloody fiasco but Hitler refused at first to allow a retreat. He poured resources into unworkable plans and failed to react quickly to changing situations.

By 1945, the Allies were closing in on Berlin. Bombs were raining down on the capital and Hitler was lurking in a bunker, but he would not consider any talk of surrender. He had faith that his 'thousand-year empire' would triumph, and was certain there were ways to still win. However, he was making plans for armies that were unable to function or no longer existed. When the Soviets entered Berlin itself, even Hitler had to admit that the war was lost, and he committed suicide to avoid being captured. The man was dead, but the memory of the evil he had done would live on long after Hitler's corpse stopped smouldering in a trench where it was set ablaze.

FRANCISCO FRANCO

Francisco Franco Bahamonde entered the world in 1892 in Spain into a relatively wealthy family. He was expected to join the navy, as previous generations of his family had, but an accident of history set him on another path. Due to the Spanish-American War of 1898, Spain found itself with a vastly reduced navy and no need for officers to man ships that did not exist. Franco decided to join the army instead.

As the youngest entry to the military academy, Franco found himself bullied by the other cadets and mocked for his diminutive stature. After graduation he was sent to Morocco in 1912, where Spain was fighting a war against the Riffians, a group of Berbers who had risen up against the Spanish presence. Spanish forces came under attack from guerrilla bands and more often than not were slaughtered due to inexperience and poor training. Franco was part of a new elite force meant to turn the tide of the war.

It was in Morocco that Franco learned the hard lessons of battle which were to mark his eventual rise to power. Despite his youth, Franco managed to earn promotion and military honours, becoming the youngest major in the Spanish army. In the next few years, he rose to lead the Spanish Foreign Legion and won the attention of the royal court in Madrid. Franco was in charge of one of the naval landings which turned the course of the Moroccan war in 1925, leading to him becoming, at thirty-three years old, the youngest general in all of Europe. After the Rif War, he was made the director of a new military academy – and he used this position to raise a generation of officers fanatically loyal to him.

The year 1931 was a turning point for Spain when an election showed widespread support for socialist and republican parties. King Alfonso XIII had always supported conservative and authoritarian policies and many Spaniards were calling for liberalization. When it seemed as if the army had also deserted the king, Alfonso left Spain and a new republic was declared. The new government acted fast to provide a revised constitution. Their changes, such as reducing the powers of the

Catholic church, might have been too fast for a country with such deeply entrenched ties to Catholicism. Franco continued to serve in the army and avoided becoming embroiled with coups being plotted by other nationalists.

The left-wing government fell following the 1933 elections. Under the centre-right government that won that year, insurrections, often bloody, sprang up as left-wing partisans attempted to stop changes being imposed. Murders of businessmen and clergy happened almost daily. Franco proved himself more than willing to use his forces to destroy anyone he perceived as a threat to European civilization – especially communists and socialists.

The violence besetting Spain polarized the public between the left (Republicans) and the right (Nationalists), and elections

THE BUTCHER OF ASTURIAS

Eduardo López Ochoa, the soldier sent by the government to put down the 1934 workers' revolt in Asturias, allowed his forces to carry out atrocities. To left-wing activists, he became a figure of hatred. At the outbreak of the Civil War, Ochoa was in hospital and, to avoid being attacked by the mob outside, had to pretend to be dead and was smuggled out in a coffin. This was broken open, however, and Ochoa was killed. His head was paraded through the streets.

in 1936 were a virtual tie. Franco, as one of the foremost soldiers in the country, was approached to take part in a military-led nationalist coup and given control of the forces in Africa. The attempted swift takeover of the country failed but left the Nationalists in control of large areas of Spain. Full-scale civil war then erupted.

Franco started by executing hundreds of soldiers who remained loyal to the republic. With support from Hitler and Mussolini, he was able to transport thousands of troops from Africa to Spain. The Soviet Union and Western socialists supported the Republican side and the civil war became a fight between world powers with Spanish lives caught in the middle.

When José Sanjurjo, who had led the attempted coup, died in a plane crash, Franco emerged as the most important of the Nationalist generals. The Civil War was marked by executions and purges on both sides, but Franco won the support of Spanish bishops to exterminate his left-wing enemies. Union leaders, Republican politicians, teachers and others were rounded up and either killed immediately or stuffed into overcrowded prisons and concentration camps. Terror was explicitly used by the Nationalists as a weapon of war. The town of Guernica was bombed and strafed by aircraft on market day when thousands of civilians were gathered together.

The Republican forces were driven back until they had no choice but to surrender in 1939. Franco, as the *generalissimo* of a country destroyed by years of brutal war, solidified his position by further butchering thousands of enemies. He also steered a course of careful friendly neutrality with the Axis powers in World War II. Though Franco was drawn towards fascist Germany and Italy, who shared his anti-communist views, Spain could ill afford more battles, so he offered only moderate military support to the Axis. After the war, Franco ruled Spain as an absolute dictator without even the fig leaf of a nominal parliament.

Spain was left as a shell of a nation – and in a difficult financial position as the United States did not offer it aid to rebuild, as it did with other European countries after World War II. Only the Cold War changed things when, in 1953, Franco allowed American air bases to be stationed in Spain in return for military and financial aid. By this point, the tens or hundreds of thousands of executions carried out by Franco's regime had slowed. Spain started to boom and foreign tourists brought in much-needed money.

Repression under Franco was enforced by armed military police ready to crack down on anyone who spoke out against him. There was even a prison filled with priests who sympathized with left-wing victims of the government. The Francoist government lasted until 1975, and near the end of his life Franco had to admit that he would need to name a successor.

Technically, Spain was a monarchy throughout much of Franco's rule – but he never said who the new king would be, so Franco remained the sole authority in the country. In 1969, Franco selected Prince Juan Carlos, a grandson of Alfonso XIII, as his successor because he believed the prince would stick to the policies Franco had enacted. Franco died in 1975 and was given a grand funeral and grander tomb. Instead of reigning as an absolute monarch, King Juan Carlos oversaw the transition of Spain back to democracy.

RAFAEL TRUJILLO

Rafael Trujillo Molina would rule over the Dominican Republic for more than thirty years as one of the most brutal dictators in the world at a time when Latin America and the Caribbean islands were infamous for dictatorships. From 1930 to 1961, under his leadership, thousands of people were executed both within the nation and outside the country on the orders of *El Jefe* – 'The Boss'.

Trujillo was born in 1891 to an ordinary lower-middle class family, but those who remembered him as a boy insisted he acted as if he was from the elite upper class. How Trujillo earned the money he felt he deserved was not something that much concerned him, even if it involved criminality. He may have learned this from his father, who supposedly supplemented his meagre income with a bit of cattle rustling.

The Dominican Republic at this time was notoriously unstable, with governments rising and falling regularly as rebellions and revolutions swept across the country. In 1916, the USA landed a force of marines to disband the rebel armies and protect American interests in the country. The US declared a military government and would occupy the Dominican Republic for the next eight years. Trujillo was trained by the American marines as part of a project to create a new national guard to bolster the occupation force's control of the country. When the Americans left in 1924, the new Dominican president Horacio Vásquez put the national guard under Trujillo's control. This proved to be a mistake.

In 1930, Vásquez faced a rebellion and called on Trujillo to crush the revolt. Trujillo had already struck a bargain with the rebels and simply stood back as the capital fell and the president fled to the American embassy. In the following elections, Trujillo stood as the only candidate after his armed men intimidated anyone who might have wanted to run against him. Understandably in these conditions, he won over 99 per cent of the vote. He ordered his new government to declare that they were living in the new Era of Trujillo.

The United States looked on this development of autocracy in the Dominican Republic with unconcern. Trujillo, with his command of the army, seemed to offer stability in the region, and the United States was decidedly isolationist in the 1930s, not wanting to become embroiled in foreign entanglements.

When Trujillo efficiently organized relief efforts after a disastrous hurricane hit the capital many on the world stage applauded his leadership. He called on aid from his old US marine friends and mobilized other sources of foreign aid, though he kept all the credit for disaster relief for himself. In the aftermath, the capital was rebuilt as Trujillo City and martial law was established throughout the country.

He maintained his leadership through bribery, naked threats of violence and fear. Those who served in the military were well paid and well supplied so that their loyalty could be depended on. In case anyone attempted to build up their own faction within the army, Trujillo made sure to shift commanders regularly to new appointments.

Soon only one political party, Trujillo's, was allowed to operate. Those who refused to join the party were at risk of arrest and those who did join the party were 'encouraged' to donate a portion of their earnings back to the government. Yet Trujillo was celebrated by many for his leadership when he modernized the economy, stabilized the currency and improved the standard of life for much of the country. In a few years, he was able to pay off the nation's debts and declare that he had completely freed it from foreign interference.

The Dominican Republic shares its island with the nation of Haiti, and Trujillo stoked hostility with the neighbouring state. In 1937, he ordered a slaughter of Haitians migrants based on rumours that Haitians were stealing cattle – something his own father had been accused of. The army was ordered to descend on Haitians, who mainly lived in the border region, and systematically exterminate them.

THE PARSLEY MASSACRE

The murder of Haitians in 1937 is often known as the Parsley Massacre because of a test which soldiers were said to force on suspected Haitians. If there were doubts about their ethnicity, people were asked to say the word *perejil* – meaning parsley – and if they failed to pronounce it 'properly', in the Dominican way, they were killed.

Reports of the massacre, targeted mostly at black Haitians, state that hundreds of people were rounded up at a time and then attacked by soldiers. Men, women and children were clubbed, hacked or bayonetted to death. Bodies were burned or simply dumped in trenches, while others were said to have been thrown into the sea. When Haitians fled towards the river which divided Haiti from the Dominican Republic they were forced into the water to drown or were killed on the banks and pushed in. Over six days of carnage, perhaps 35,000 people died.

Trujillo did not always maintain his role as president and sometimes allowed others to take the position, though they were never anything but puppets for him. Even when not officially in power, a cult of personality persisted around Trujillo: monuments and slogans were erected across the country and everything from mountains to parks were named after him. Signs could be seen in most homes saying 'In this house Trujillo is Chief'. Churches were forced to put up signs which declared that God ruled in heaven but Trujillo ruled on Earth.

The terror of the Trujillo regime was not limited to his own country. The secret service, known as SIM, patrolled the streets and enforced his rule through close monitoring of every aspect of a person's life. In 1956, Jesús Galíndez, a critic of Trujillo, disappeared from the streets of New York and is presumed to have been captured and killed by the secret service. When several Catholic bishops spoke of easing the political repression, Trujillo is said to have considered ordering the assassination of the pope. SIM was responsible for tens of thousands of murders and disappearances.

By 1960, the repressive Trujillo government was breeding more dissidents than it could round up. The United States was also encouraging democratic reforms in the Dominican Republic. In 1961, a group of eight conspirators ambushed Trujillo's car as he was being driven to meet his young mistress. They riddled the car with gunshots and Trujillo bled to death.

The regime did not die with the dictator, however. Those in power were able to capture and kill the assassins while many other people were arrested and tortured to find out how far the conspiracy went. Trujillo's son Ramfis slid into his father's place but proved less able to maintain control. He was forced to flee the same year, taking his father's coffin, which was said to be lined with valuables.

MAO ZEDONG

When a tyrant attempts to create a new and better version of their society it often comes with a heavy death toll. No dictator in history may have killed more of his own people than Chairman Mao Zedong of China. Under his leadership, millions died,

with estimates ranging from 30 to 70 million, as China went from an agrarian society towards superpower status.

Mao Zedong was born in 1893 to a mildly prosperous farming family in central China. During his formative years, many people from more elite backgrounds shunned him as a country bumpkin, but his ambition would drive him towards power.

As a young man, Mao studied vociferously and read widely, considering himself to be somewhat more intellectual than the people around him. He understood the need for Chinese society to modernize if it was to compete on the world stage, and flirted with various different political theories on how to bring this about. While at school, he formed a revolutionary society but it was only following a move to Beijing in 1917, where he worked as a librarian, that he became attached to the doctrines of Marxism. In 1921, he was present at the first congress of the Chinese Communist Party. At first, the communists agreed to work with other parties to bring about a revolution against the warlords running large areas of China. Their shared long-term aim was to create a strong, unified China free from foreign influence.

Mao's travels across the country to learn more about how land was distributed left him with the idea that even those with a relatively small amount of land would oppose the revolution he planned. On the other hand, he felt that millions of peasants could be turned into a force to support communism, an idea that was mocked at the time. In 1927, the Nationalist

Party (KMT) led by Chiang Kai-shek turned against the communists. Tens of thousands of communists were killed. In the civil war that followed, Mao helped to organize the communist forces.

In 1934, when cornered by the KMT, the communists had to escape by undergoing the Long March. Mao was elected to lead the 100,000 refugees on a perilous path over 10,000 kilometres: only around 8,000 people survived at the end of the journey.

When the Japanese invaded China, Mao and his forces agreed to work again with the nationalist government to oppose the invaders. The communist Red Army under Mao swelled in size and proved effective at fighting the Japanese. After the war ended, Mao fielded around a million men in his People's Liberation Army, which then fought another civil war against the KMT. Hundreds of thousands of people died during sieges of cities, quite apart from in pitched battles. At the end of 1949, Chiang Kai-shek fled from mainland China to Taiwan. Mao was now undisputed master of the People's Republic of China and received help from the Soviet Union.

He began to change Chinese society at once. Under land law reforms, teams of communists toured the countryside to identify landlords and abolish rents placed on peasants. The worst landlords, labelled as tyrants, were put on trial. Mao encouraged peasants to kill landlords because by bloodying their hands they would be tied to the revolution. More than half a million landlords were killed and millions more were placed into labour camps. Women did enjoy greater freedom than under the previous regime due to a belief in the equality of the sexes.

The Chinese population was growing rapidly and yet agricultural production failed to keep up with increasing demand. Mao decided that a revolution within the revolution was required. The Great Leap Forward began in 1958 with the collectivization of farms, where all would work for the good of all. Without calling on expert advice, policies were enacted with unexpected results. When people were encouraged to slaughter sparrows on the grounds that they ate grain, it led to an explosion in the population of locusts which sparrows also eat. The resulting locust swarms contributed to the great famine that killed somewhere between 20 to 50 million. Attempts to revitalize the steel industry by building backyard furnaces to make steel on a small scale resulted in millions of tonnes of unusable metal.

Mao wanted China to modernize, and used Soviet aid to construct infrastructure such as dams in Henan province in central China. Many of these were not fit for purpose. In 1975, a typhoon contributed to the collapse of several dams, and the flood which resulted caused the deaths of up to 250,000 people.

After the Great Leap Forward proved to be a backward step, Mao himself stepped back to allow others to take part in the leadership, but in 1966 he renewed his power by launching the Cultural Revolution against supposed enemies of the revolution. To show that he was still in the peak of health and very much in charge, Mao staged a swim in the Yangtze river, even as human waste floated around him. The Cultural Revolution would make Mao the indisputable leader by activating the masses against his enemies in the party. The cult of personality of Mao had long been evolving, and in 1966, he explained his theories in what became known as the Little Red Book, which became the emblem of his rule.

MAO MANGOES

When Mao was given some special mangoes by the Pakistani foreign ministry, he passed them along to his 'Worker-Peasant Mao Zedong Thought Propaganda Teams'. The mangoes, with their touch of the Mao magic, became too valuable to eat so they were preserved as symbols of the great leader's love for his people. One mango was boiled in a huge vat of water so that many people could enjoy a spoonful of the resulting liquid. The mangoes were paraded with great fanfare. Wax models of the fruit were made for workers to stare at and revere. Propaganda hailed the wonders of mangoes, and mango-themed products from soap to cigarettes became all the rage.

The Cultural Revolution saw gangs of indoctrinated students and members of the Red Guard youth movement physically attack anyone denounced as part of the bourgeoisie. Anything, or anyone, thought to represent pre-revolutionary ideas was destroyed. At 'struggle sessions', enemies of the state were paraded in front of howling crowds and humiliated, beaten and sometimes killed. Millions of young people from the cities were sent to the countryside to work as peasants in harsh conditions to be re-educated as good communist citizens. It is unknown how many people died before the Cultural Revolution was brought to an end following Mao's death.

Chairman Mao died in 1976 after suffering from several ailments for years. His preserved body is still on display in a memorial hall in Tiananmen Square.

NICOLAE CEAUȘESCU

. . . .

In 1918, Nicolae Ceaușescu was born in Romania to a peasant family with only a small area of land to tend and a handful of farm animals to call their own. In the aftermath of World War I, Romania found itself caught between the rising Soviet regime in Russia and fascist parties at home. Nicolae chose to side with the communists and was active from the age of fourteen, used as a party tool for small assignments.

His communist tendencies soon brought him to the attention of the authorities, who feared that the communists would destabilize the democracy and hand the state over to the Soviets. Multiple arrests followed and mugshots of the baby-faced Ceaușescu can still be found. Although he was only a teenager, he was viewed as an agitator and a dangerously subversive communist, and was sentenced to several years in prison.

It was when Ceaușescu emerged from prison in 1939 that he met one of the most important people in his life – his future wife Elena. She was also from a peasant family and had recently joined the Communist Party. By all accounts, theirs was a true love match and the pair would work closely together for the rest of their lives.

World War II saw Ceaușescu arrested and imprisoned repeatedly by a government that was initially neutral but soon leaned ever more closely to the Axis powers. His time behind bars brought him into contact with high-ranking communists and Ceaușescu made himself useful to them by acting as their thuggish enforcer.

In 1941, Romania's fascist government joined in the Nazi invasion of the Soviet Union, and in the disastrous aftermath, Romania found the Red Army counter-attacking. A communist-backed coup drove out the fascists and Romania switched sides, but this did not stop Soviet forces marching into the country. When the dust settled after the Allied victory, Romania found itself occupied, and its monarchy was swept away to be replaced by a republic under communist control. Ceaușescu's rise to power had begun.

Ceaușescu moved swiftly up through the ranks of the Communist Party which was under the leadership of Gheorghe Gheorghiu-Dej, who had been one of Ceaușescu's closest allies in prison. Gheorghiu-Dej ruled Romania from 1952 until his death in 1965. There were other communist leaders who might have had a better claim to taking power at that point, but in the in-fighting that followed, Ceaușescu took control.

Ceaușescu might have seemed a safe pair of hands who would continue the policies of his predecessor, but in some ways he proved more radical. He feared that Romania had a chronic lack of manpower and decided to increase the population by banning abortion and contraception, and making divorce ever harder. Though births increased dramatically, many families were unable to support their larger families and Romanian orphanages, often with horrific conditions, swelled to breaking point.

Soviet forces had left Romania in 1958 and Ceaușescu continued to separate Romania from the Soviet Union. This won him praise from Romanians and Western leaders who saw Romanian independence as a useful split in the Soviet sphere. Ceaușescu, the former peasant, found himself fêted on international trips as a statesman able to bridge the divide of the Cold War.

It was one trip abroad that really changed Ceaușescu's methods of government. In 1971, he went to North Korea and was greeted by thousands of people lining the streets, all of whom had been drilled to loudly proclaim their love for him and dance in unison. Ceaușescu was impressed at the level of control the dictator Kim Il Sung had over his people, as well as his independence from foreign influence. On his return to Romania, Ceaușescu decided he needed a cult of personality of his own.

Ceaușescu sought to reorganize Romania with a miniature cultural revolution. Censorship, which he had earlier on relaxed, was now strictly enforced. Only artistic productions that celebrated the communist regime and Ceaușescu himself were allowed. Young people were to be indoctrinated from birth on the glories of Ceaușescu's brilliant leadership and later

PRESIDENTIAL FINERY

In a communist regime, where everyone is supposed to be equal, it can be hard for a leader to properly display their power. In 1974, Ceaușescu named himself the first president of Romania and had a sceptre crafted to mark his new position and to echo those used by monarchs. When Salvador Dalí sent a mocking telegram congratulating Ceaușescu on his new bauble, the communist press loudly trumpeted the message, having completely missed the artist's irony.

put to work building all the infrastructure the leader wanted. Anyone who breached the laws of the new Romania would be sentenced to lengthy periods in prison.

Ceaușescu and his wife Elena were showered with honours and grand titles by his cronies. Ceaușescu's writings were widely published and studied as the works of a genius who had finally perfected the communist system. Romanian intellectuals of all fields were expected to contribute to the books of praise produced each year. Even as Romania became more repressive, Ceaușescu continued to be lauded by Western leaders as a 'good' communist. Some of the welcomes he received were grudging. On a state visit to the United Kingdom, Queen Elizabeth II is said to have hidden in a bush on the grounds of Buckingham Palace to avoid having to exchange small talk with the Ceaușescus.

Romania was being rebuilt on a grand scale that the government could ill afford. Uniform concrete buildings were ordered for cities and villages, creating a concrete jungle. Vast areas of Bucharest were flattened when Ceaușescu decided to build a huge palace for himself with hundreds and hundreds of rooms and a nuclear-war-proof bunker. Meanwhile, ordinary Romanians were suffering from food and fuel shortages and a vicious secret police.

By 1989, the writing was on the wall for communist regimes throughout Europe. Student demonstrations emerged across Romania and troops were ordered to fire on them. On 21 December, hoping to show he was still in complete control,

Ceaușescu bussed thousands of people into Bucharest to view him giving a speech. But just moments into the speech, the spectators began screaming and shouting at him, and Ceaușescu fell into impotent silence. The crowds soon rioted through the streets: Ceaușescu's rule was crumbling.

The Ceaușescus remained in the city as it descended into chaos and military commanders refused to follow his orders. They were stuffed into a helicopter to flee as a mob stormed the palace. When the helicopter was forced down by the military, the couple were bundled into a room and locked there as others decided their fates.

On 25 December, Ceaușescu and his wife were placed on trial by a military tribunal and charged with crimes relating to their decades in power. There was never any doubt of the judgment or the punishment. Both were found guilty and sentenced to death. They were hauled out of the court, their heads covered, and shot by a firing squad as television cameras recorded the end of the Ceaușescu regime.

FIDEL CASTRO

During the Cold War, the USA was never afraid to interfere with another nation's government if they threatened to turn communist. Financial, diplomatic and military pressure were

all applied to foreign countries – wherever they were in the world – to keep them on the side of democracy. If these failed, then a well-timed coup could usually be initiated to bring them back into the fold. When Cuba, just ninety miles from the United States itself, turned communist in the 1960s it nearly led to global apocalypse.

Fidel Castro, born in 1926, had a relatively privileged upbringing and might have enjoyed a middle-class life after studying law at Havana University. It was while at university, though, that Castro became a staunch opponent of US imperialist policies and a supporter of communism. He rose to lead the student union and delivered fiery speeches. Many people dabble in student politics but Castro got a taste for leading crowds.

Castro campaigned for the populist Party of the Cuban People in the Cuban presidential elections of 1948. His candidate lost, and Castro grew disenchanted with hopes of peaceful change when Fulgencio Batista overthrew the elected government and ruled as a dictator from 1952. Castro gathered a small force of about 160 men to fight against Batista and hoped to lead an uprising by attacking a military base in 1953. The government fought off the rebels and Castro was captured. At his trial, he delivered one of his masterpiece speeches in which he declared that history would absolve him whatever judgment the court reached. Despite being sentenced to a lengthy prison stay, Castro was allowed to go into exile in Mexico in 1955.

The following year, Castro returned, leading a small group of revolutionaries, including Che Guevara, to wage a guerrilla campaign against the Batista regime. After years of bloody fighting, Batista fled Cuba in 1959 and the rebels were able to claim victory. Castro chose the liberal Manuel Urrutia as the new president for Cuba, but he was effectively just a figurehead. Castro remained in charge of the armed forces and in short order became the prime minister. He then took almost all power into his own hands, postponing promised elections indefinitely.

Castro supported the executions of those accused of shoring up the Batista government, and used his authority to place communists into positions of power to undermine those who hoped for a new democratic regime. Communist policies such as limiting ownership of land and nationalization of industries were introduced. When President Urrutia attempted to curb Castro's changes, Castro's supporters drove him out and Castro named a new president more in line with his beliefs. Many of Castro's policies, like improving educational opportunities and lowering rents, were hugely popular.

The United States became increasingly hostile to Castro, while disaffected people around the world began to think of him as a liberator and saviour of the poor from imperialism. President John F. Kennedy supported the CIA's arming of Cuban rebels to launch an invasion of Cuba to overthrow Castro in 1961. This Bay of Pigs invasion was a debacle and the attempted rebels were captured, embarrassing Kennedy that the United States was not able to deal with a small island nation on its doorstep. It also drove Castro to closer ties with the Soviet Union.

In 1962, the Soviets began constructing missile sites on Cuba which would allow them to strike the United States with nuclear weapons, triggering the Cuban Missile Crisis. For the Soviets, this was a balancing of the military scales, while for the United States, this was an existential crisis. The Soviets believed that once the missiles were in place there would be nothing the Americans could do to remove them. Kennedy ordered a blockade of Cuba to stop more weapons arriving. Soviet and American ships came close to fighting over the issue and many in America thought it would be impossible to avoid a nuclear war at this point. Only the fact that the Soviets turned their ships around and agreed to remove their missiles saved the world at that moment.

ASSASSINATION ATTEMPTS

The American authorities were keen to get rid of Castro in any way possible. Plans were made to make him appear out of control by lacing him with hallucinogens before a speech or poisoning his shoes with thallium to cause his famous beard to fall out. Other attempts to kill Castro ranged from the simple gunshot to the cartoonishly absurd. As he was an avid diver, plots were drawn up to blow him up with an exploding seashell or coat his diving suit with toxins. Given his ability to survive all assassination attempts, Castro would joke that he was impossible to kill.

Castro had not enjoyed being a plaything caught between the squabbling Soviets and the United States and from then on would attempt to maintain a more independent role in world affairs. However, American embargoes on Cuban trade left him with little choice but to rely on Soviet aid. When the Soviet Union started to unravel in the late 1990s, it seemed as if change would finally have to come to Cuba, but, unlike many communist leaders at this time, Castro was able to survive the shift in world politics. He looked to new allies in the rising socialist leaders of Latin America and was able to maintain a level of economic growth.

Castro's control of Cuba may have brought several advances such as reducing racial discrimination and improving hygiene and access to medical care. But a dictator cannot exert control without limiting the power of others. At any given time, there were tens of thousands of political prisoners jailed for any action thought to be against the Castro regime. Prisoners were often tortured and many were put into labour camps. Those who the government judged to be guilty, as suspects always were before they were arrested, would find themselves being seized from their homes at night before being rushed through a trial and straight into a prison.

Fidel Castro's rule of Cuba lasted from 1959 to 2008. He managed to cling onto power and outlive many of his opponents thanks to the machinery of control that he had constructed early in his reign, which limited the opportunity for anyone to voice opposition to him. It seemed as if Castro would never fall from power.

However, after one of Castro's legendarily lengthy speeches he tumbled from a stage in 2004 and broke multiple bones. It seemed as if age was finally catching up with him. But even then he managed to maintain control for four more years. He recovered from his injuries, including internal bleeding, and once again seemed immortal. In 2008, however, Castro finally retired from office. Power did not leave the Castro family, though, as he handed the leadership over to his younger brother Raúl – a relative spring chicken at just seventy-five years old.

Fidel Castro died in 2016, years after George W. Bush had predicted: 'One day the good Lord will take Fidel Castro away.' Perhaps God waited so long because he feared he lacked the patience for one of Castro's interminable orations.

FRANÇOIS DUVALIER

Doctors swear an oath to 'first do no harm' but history is littered with medical professionals who have inflicted pain on innumerable people. François 'Papa Doc' Duvalier, president of Haiti from 1957 to 1971, was one such doctor. Under his rule, terror and murder were among the tools he applied surgically to control people and extract untold wealth from his country.

François Duvalier was born in 1907 and early on chose to dedicate his life to medicine. The course of his life was changed by the presence of United States military authorities who arrived in Haiti in 1915. When the Haitian president Guillaume Sam was assassinated earlier that year, the US feared that the loans that it had extended to Haiti were at risk of remaining unpaid. So they sent in the army and placed officials in key positions.

To many black Haitians it seemed as if they were slipping back into slavery when their new American overlords treated them with disdain, while lighter-skinned Haitians had more power and thus more money.

During this time, Duvalier developed an interest in black nationalism in Haiti as well as in the African traditions the Haitians' ancestors had brought when carried across the Atlantic as slaves. Haitian Vodou was a religion which had grown through the confluence of Christianity and African faiths and Duvalier championed it as a response to imperialism. In the 1940s, the Catholic church tried and failed to wipe out belief in Vodou.

The American authorities offered Duvalier an opportunity when they expanded medical facilities and attempted to wipe out a painful tropical infection, widespread at the time, called yaws. Yaws begins with hard nodules developing on the body, which often become ulcerous and can distort bone – meaning yaws can disfigure or even kill. Duvier was given the chance to study in America to take part in the campaign to eradicate the disease. On his return, he travelled across Haiti, treating the poor communities where yaws was endemic and blighted the lives of the majority of people. To these patients, he became known as the friendly and accomplished 'Papa Doc' whom they travelled miles to visit in hopes of a cure.

From 1946, Duvalier was appointed to several important government positions under President Dumarsais Estimé. But when Estimé was overthrown in 1950 by a military coup,

Duvalier fled to the countryside and became one of the leaders of the opposition. People who knew Duvalier at this time said that he closely studied Machiavelli's *The Prince* and cultivated a deep mistrust of anyone who might betray him to the authorities, who were trying to hunt him down. The fall of the military-backed leadership in 1956 allowed Duvalier to return to government, and in 1957, he was elected to the presidency.

Duvalier's victory was contested by his opponent and violence broke out, but Duvalier was able to call on his brutal supporters who were already organizing into a potent paramilitary force. These men, known for hiding their faces behind hoods, were used to break up strikes and protests. Duvalier also hit back by arresting his enemies and rounding up any potential dissidents. Political parties other than his own were banned.

The black nationalist movement and popular support for Duvalier threatened the position of the mixed-race elites who had traditionally held most political power. In 1958, a group of military officers, together with some American mercenaries, staged a coup to restore the previous social power structure to Haiti. The attempt failed almost immediately when soldiers showed no enthusiasm for rebellion. In any case, the majority of people supported Papa Doc's social changes that gave more help to black people. The rebels were killed, but Duvalier became ever more distrustful. He now created a paramilitary group called the Volunteers for National Security who were loyal only to him; history would know these people as the feared Tontons Macoutes.

UNCLE GUNNYSACK

The Tontons Macoutes were named for a figure from Haitian folklore also known as Uncle Gunnysack. He was a man who stalked the night with a bag and when he found a naughty boy or girl he would stuff them into his bag. Such children would never be seen again. Opponents of Duvalier would be taken from their home at night and disappear forever in the same way, making the name of Duvalier's thugs a grim joke.

Duvalier had learned to fear the power of the army, and so expanded the Tontons Macoutes until they dwarfed the military. Members of the organization had the right to strike, murder or rape almost any Haitian at any time. When Duvalier suffered a heart attack in 1959, the leader of the Tontons Macoutes, Clément Barbot, was temporarily placed in charge of Haiti. After Duvalier recovered, he believed Barbot had tried to depose him, and had Barbot arrested. Duvalier's doctor thought the dictator might have suffered brain damage during his illness, which made him even more unpredictable.

When Barbot was released and started to plot to kidnap Duvalier's children, a manhunt for Barbot began. Duvalier was convinced that Barbot had the ability to transform into a black dog and so ordered the slaying of all black dogs in Haiti.

Barbot was tracked down while hiding in a field, so Duvalier's men set it ablaze and shot him as he fled. Duvalier treasured the photograph of Barbot's corpse.

Duvalier's people knew how to please him by bringing evidence of their ruthless activities. When a suspected communist agitator was killed, his head was cut off and delivered to Duvalier as a trophy. The bodies of those slain by the Tontons Macoutes would often be left on public display as a bloody lesson to anyone who might even think of objecting to Duvalier's rule. It was said that Duvalier enjoyed watching his torturers inflict horrific pain on enemies. Tens of thousands of Haitians were killed or disappeared, and many more fled into exile to escape the regime.

The cruel regime of Duvalier might have drawn the ire of the United States, but he came to power at the right time. With Cuba under the communist Fidel Castro, the Americans wanted an ally in the region. Their money helped to prop up Duvalier – as did his personal monopoly on tobacco. Bribes were widely distributed to keep many loyal, while fear of the Tontons Macoutes controlled the rest of the people. Duvalier was keen to be seen as a generous man and would dole out wads of paper money to the public in heavily publicized events.

Duvalier seems to have been popular with his people, if the election results of 1963 are to be believed. More than 1,300,000 votes were cast in his favour and not a single vote was recorded against him. A later referendum with similar levels of support gave Duvalier the title of President for Life. It seemed fortunate for Haiti that life would not be long for Duvalier. His health was never good and he died of a stroke in 1971.

Unfortunately, power passed immediately to his son Jean-Claude, known as Baby Doc, even though he was just nineteen years old. Under the rule of the playboy Baby Doc, Haiti would suffer many more years of pain.

POL POT

. . . .

Born in Cambodia in 1925, Pol Pot enjoyed a relatively comfortable youth. His family were farmers and one of his cousins was a lover of the Cambodian king. Pot received an education, studied Buddhism and went to live in the capital, Phnom Penh, with his well-connected cousin. All of this is darkly ironic given the holocaust he would inflict on his nation, in which many with his background would be slaughtered.

At this time, Cambodia was under the control of France, and in 1949, Pol Pot was privileged enough to be selected to study in Paris. It was there that he became involved in Marxist politics and communism. Stalinist and Maoist texts, with all the strength of those leaders, appealed to Pot. Communism seemed to offer the hope of Cambodia throwing off the shackles of its French imperialist protectors.

When Pot returned to Cambodia in 1953, he found his country descending into civil war. With several of his friends, he joined a communist rebel group for which, at first, he just undertook farming and cooking duties. Then, the Cambodian king, Sihanouk, was able to gain independence from France that year and peace began to diminish the chances of rebel success. Pol Pot was forced to support himself by becoming a teacher, by all accounts a good one, but continued to be active in Marxist circles.

The twists and turns of Cambodian politics in the decade that followed are too complex to expand on here. Pol Pot rose to became one of the leaders of the group that would be renamed the Communist Party of Kampuchea (a native name for the country), known to their opponents as the Khmer Rouge. He travelled to China to gain the support of the Chinese communist regime and, in 1968, the Khmer Rouge launched an insurrection against King Sihanouk. When his government used brutal tactics to put down the communists, it only bolstered support for Pol Pot. Large parts of the country fell to the Marxist forces, who implemented harsh laws against financial corruption and moral deviancy, as they saw it. Land was seized from successful farmers and handed out to the poor. It was an early sign of the nation Pol Pot wanted to build – an agrarian one where people lived off the land in Stalinist bliss.

By 1975, the forces of the Khmer Rouge were closing in on the capital. As soon as Phnom Penh fell, Pol Pot ordered the arrest and execution of people associated with the former government. It was also decided that the two million inhabitants would leave the corrupt city and go to work on the land. Within hours of Khmer forces entering the city, they were ordering people to leave. Soldiers with guns marched everyone, from children in schools to patients in hospital, onto the roads, which soon jammed. Anyone who fought back, or even argued against leaving, was cut down in a spray of bullets. Thousands died as the cities of Cambodia were turned into ghost towns and more died on the long walk into the countryside.

People who had only ever lived in the city were commanded to till fields, gather crops, dig canals and work on building projects. Though the aim was to create a society without class, the Khmer Rouge divided its people into 'old citizens', who had supported them from the start, and 'new citizens', those driven out of the cities.

Pol Pot declared that history had been reset by his victory and there was no time to waste in creating his new utopia. First, all vestiges of the old order had to be swept away. On the collective farms, victims were picked out for the most innocuous of reasons. Wearing glasses or knowing how to speak another language marked a person out as a dangerous subversive, as they might be an intellectual with contacts abroad. Monks were labelled as parasites on the state. To save on bullets, many were beaten to death with farm tools – being burned alive was also cost effective for the Khmer Rouge. To encourage other workers, bodies were left in the open.

Conditions on work sites were primitive. Diseases ran rampant and there was little medicine to be found. Epidemics killed thousands. Pot's attempts to control agricultural production simply sparked food shortages which condemned even more to a slow and lingering death from starvation. Those who tried to feed their families or themselves by stealing a little food were punished as traitors who were sabotaging the state.

It was not only society that needed to be reorganized, it was the individuals who made up that society. Citizens were discouraged from showing such simple acts as familial affection or crying over the punishments inflicted on them. Private property was abolished. Use of the word 'I' instead of the communist 'we' was almost a crime. For those suspected of failing to join the revolution sufficiently enthusiastically, there were hundreds of new prisons and punishment centres set up across the country. One prison, the headquarters of the ironically named 'Peace Keepers', saw tens of thousands of people pass through its doors. Fewer than ten people are known to have survived their stay there.

The Khmer Rouge ruled Cambodia for just four years before being driven out in 1979 by an invasion from Vietnam. During that short period, it is thought that up to three million Cambodians were either killed or died as a result of Pol Pot's policy. The genocide inflicted on Cambodia by Pol Pot ranks as one of the worst crimes against humanity in the twentieth century. Since the fall of the Khmer Rouge, more than 20,000 mass graves have been identified in what became known as the 'killing fields'.

Pol Pot did not meekly give up his power and instead set up a new base of operations from which to fight back. The Khmer Rouge might have lost the capital, but large parts of the nation were still under its control and they continued to mount guerrilla attacks on the Vietnamese and the new pro-Vietnam government. The civil war would rumble on until the late 1990s.

The failure of his regime did not see Pol Pot ousted from his position as leader of the Khmer Rouge, though he did start to suggest that he had been misled by others into too extreme a policy. His newfound gentleness did not, however, stop him ordering executions whenever he decided. In 1997, the end of the Khmer Rouge was in sight and Pol Pot was surrounded by rebellious members of his own party. He was by this time partially paralysed by a stroke and had to be carried away from an enemy attack, but was caught and placed under arrest. He denied accusations of being responsible for millions of deaths.

There can be no sufficient punishment for Pol Pot's crimes but he escaped imprisonment in 1998 by dying in his sleep. His body was burned on a pile of tyres. The bones of his victims are displayed in many places to remind people of the costs of following tyrannical ideologues.

IDI AMIN

. . . .

Following World War II, the British Empire was effectively dead, but its corpse continued to thrash around and cause harm. Countries which had been colonized by the United Kingdom declared themselves independent, but in many cases rapidly fell into despotism.

Uganda, where Idi Amin Dada Oumee was born in 1928, had been a British protectorate for more than thirty years, and it was in British service that Idi Amin began his rise to power. His father had fought in the British army in World War I and his mother was said to be a folk priestess and magical healer. Many of the stories about Idi Amin's childhood – such as him really being the son of a king or, as a baby, surviving alone in the jungle for days – have the feel of a fairy tale.

In 1946, Amin joined the King's African Rifles in the British army as a cook but saw action in several imperial wars including suppressing the Mau Mau rebels of Kenya. He rose through the ranks quickly. When Uganda gained independence in 1962, his rise was even more precipitous and he soon became the deputy commander of the Ugandan army.

Amin served under Prime Minister Milton Obote and was enmeshed in a financial scandal in 1965. Obote was strongly opposed to the leadership of the Democratic Republic of the Congo and offered support to rebels in the country. In return for weapons, the rebels paid Obote and his associates with gold, cash and other trade goods. Some of this money, worth hundreds of thousands of pounds today, turned up mysteriously in a bank account owned by Idi Amin. Moves were made in parliament to remove Amin, and Obote was accused of protecting him for fear of what Amin would reveal if put on trial. Obote responded by ousting the president, taking that role for himself, and appointing Amin as head of all armed forces in Uganda.

This position did not last long. When President Obote was shot in the face by a would-be assassin, he cracked down on potential rivals and banned the expression of opposition to his leadership. Amin, who had been building support among certain ethnic groups, was demoted as Obote took personal control of the military. When it seemed as if charges were about to be brought against Amin on further accusations of embezzlement, Amin decided he could do a better job of running the country – it was time for a coup.

Uganda was ready for a strongman leader, as Obote was already mired in scandal and people were sick of politicians who seemed to only work for personal enrichment. The world was also ready for a coup as Obote had supported African independence movements, a stance which annoyed the British government. In 1971, while President Obote was out of the country, Amin's forces struck and took control of the streets, airports and military bases of Uganda. Obote's forces were routed and Amin had supreme control – his enemies were soon being purged from military and civilian life, often violently.

FAILED FIGHTBACK

Obote moved to Tanzania to gather Ugandan exiles and military support to overthrow Amin. The plan was to steal a plane, load it with soldiers and fly to Uganda for a swift coup. Unfortunately, the pilot was inexperienced and nearly crashed the stolen plane. Around 1,000 rebels crossed into Uganda, but Amin's forces had been alerted by the plane theft and were ready for them. When the people of Uganda also failed to rise up to support Obote, his troops were forced to retreat.

To the world, Amin came to be a figure of fun. He was grandiose, funny, sometimes stupid, sometimes cunning and he made ridiculous statements. He declared himself to be 'Conqueror of the British Empire in Africa in General and Uganda in Particular'. Amin enjoyed sending messages to world leaders, particularly Queen Elizabeth II. One note to Her Majesty said, 'I would like you to arrange for me to visit Scotland, Ireland and Wales to meet the heads of revolutionary movements fighting against your imperialist oppression.'

Another brief missive to 'Liz' invited her to visit Uganda if she wanted to meet a real man. He even asked for a pair of her underwear. When Britain experienced a recession, Amin started an ironic campaign to raise funds to rescue the British.

The people of Uganda would soon come to fear their mercurial ruler. One of Amin's first acts was to shut down Obote's unpopular secret police, but this was swiftly followed by setting up his own fearsome intelligence unit. People were stolen from the streets by agents and carried to torture chambers beneath the main building of the secret police. There, victims might be electrocuted, have their skin torn off or eyes gouged out. The lucky ones were executed soon after such torture.

Amin stoked racial and ethnic tensions within Uganda. He targeted killings against ethnic groups who had supported Obote. He used anti-Semitic rhetoric and allowed a hijacked plane carrying many Israeli passengers to land in Entebbe. The hostages were eventually freed by an Israeli raid. In 1972, he declared that the South Asians who had come to Uganda under British rule were stealing money from the country and gave around 60,000 of them ninety days to get out. Those forced to flee could only take a small amount of money with them and everything else was stolen by the Ugandan state. Many of the abandoned businesses and properties found their way into the hands of Amin supporters as bribes. Since so much economic activity had been driven by Asians, the economy of Uganda nearly collapsed.

As people suffered economically, they began to turn against their funny but terrible ruler. Rumours were widespread that Amin partook in bizarre rituals like feasting on the flesh of his murdered enemies. Amin would later claim that he did not like the taste of human meat as it was too salty. Over the course of his rule, it is thought around 300,000 Ugandans were killed by Amin's regime. So many bodies piled up that some were thrown into rivers to be eaten by crocodiles.

Those who rule by the army are often deposed by the army. Amin had a falling out with one of his generals whose supporters rose in mutinies when their leader was dismissed. When Amin's armed forces strayed into Tanzania, the Tanzanians sent a counter-invasion. Amin was forced to flee into exile. As a Muslim, Amin was able to find refuge in Saudi Arabia, and it was from there that he attempted to reconquer Uganda in 1989. But there was little support for him and he ended up back in Saudi Arabia for the rest of his life. Amin died peacefully in 2003 without ever facing punishment for his crimes.

FRANCISCO MACÍAS NGUEMA

Whether the extraordinary position of a dictator brings out the madder aspects of a person or whether only the mentally unbalanced seek ultimate power is a moot point. It is certainly true that many tyrants are dangerously eccentric, but fewer have been more insane than Francisco Macías Nguema of Equatorial Guinea.

Macías, as he became known, was born in Spanish Guinea in 1924 and, like some other despots, his early life is shrouded in mystery. It has been claimed that his father was a traditional healer who performed human sacrifice, including of Macías' brother. What is known is that he started to work for the Spanish colonial office in the 1930s and was rewarded with several positions of mid-level authority.

While other African politicians were arguing vociferously for immediate independence of their nations, Macías appeared to be keen to work with the Spanish to slowly free his country from colonial control. It was at a conference in Spain that Macías' questionable grasp on reality was first revealed. Unprompted, he started to declare that Hitler had intended to be the saviour of Africa, that he wanted to end colonialism across the globe, and merely accidentally set out to conquer Europe after deciding to eradicate Jewish people. Despite such outbursts, the Spanish were impressed with Nguema and he continued to rise to ever more important positions. He was made deputy prime minister of the autonomous government in the run-up to independence in 1964.

In the first elections of a free, renamed Equatorial Guinea, Macías was Spain's favoured candidate for president, and he was given speeches to read out. His instability, however, meant that he often wandered off-topic and simply ended up promising voters everything from homes to wives if they supported him. Unsurprisingly, these wild campaign giveaways proved popular, and Macías was elected president.

The independence movement had bolstered nationalism in Equatorial Guinea and soon there was an air of violence against the former Spanish overlords. Macías would appear on television to shout and rant against the crimes of the Spanish. He also feared plots, backed by the Spanish, to overthrow him. Spanish residents were evacuated from the country by Spain for their own safety.

Macías claimed that Atanasio Ndongo Miyone, one his rivals in the election who had been made foreign minister, was involved in a coup attempt. Official statements claimed that Miyone had come to the palace with armed troops but Macías bravely fought them off with his bare hands. Macías threw Miyone out of a window and, according to some accounts, as he lay dying on the street, pictures were taken of his death agonies for Macías' later enjoyment. Other reports say Miyone was simply arrested, tortured for days and then hanged in his prison cell. Bonifacio Ondó Edú, another rival in the election, fled the country to avoid retribution. Unfortunately, he was sent back by Spain and promptly murdered.

One of Macías' next moves was to attack the constitution, which he considered to have been imposed on him by the Spanish. By revoking the constitution, he was able to be made president for life and ban all political parties other than his own. If even a single person in a village was thought to be a rebel, Macías would order the burning of every home and the execution of everyone there.

CHRISTMAS MASSACRES

In 1969, Macías is said to have forced more than 150 political opponents into a stadium. To the sound of one of Macías' favourite songs, Mary Hopkin's 'Those Were the Days', they were publicly executed. Accounts of this event vary. Some say the executioners were dressed as Father Christmas to add a festive aspect to the proceedings. A UN report says thirty-six of the prisoners were buried up to their necks and then bitten to death by ants.

By 1974, the majority of those who had been elected to the parliament of 1968 had been either killed or simply disappeared, never to reappear. Suspicion was a way of life for Macías, and soon the entire nation learned to either support the president's mania for catching traitors or risk being rounded up themselves. Advancement and rewards were offered to those who informed on spies and opposition parties. Neighbours and families had to distrust each other for fear of being named and being bundled away into prisons and a shallow grave.

Prisoners would not often be granted the luxury of a trial and even behind bars they could not escape suspicion of treachery. In 1974, those held in Bata prison were thought to be plotting a coup – somehow – and so were promptly beaten to death with clubs. A few were granted a trial to allow the coup attempt to be proved, but even in a court of law, truth was in limited supply. There were few judges and lawyers not in the service of Macías, so the outcome was a foregone conclusion. The accused had defence lawyers who asked the court to impose the death penalty on their own clients.

People cannot live under conditions like these for long. Wherever possible, they started to flee the country. Macías destroyed the major roads out of the country by digging trenches filled with spikes to block them. When people turned to boats to escape, he banned the fishing industry to stop fugitives having access to the sea.

After 1974, Macías became so paranoid and fearful of assassination that he left his palace and capital to live exclusively in a fort surrounded by his military. To ensure he would be the only source of patronage, he carried the entire money supply of the country with him to his new home. Macías began to have delusions of his own importance and added impressive and meaningless titles after his own name. At first, churches had to declare that God had created Equatorial Guinea thanks to Macías. Eventually, this was changed to 'There is no other god than Macías', and organized religions were banned.

With an unstable dictator making increasingly bizarre orders such as executing so-called 'intellectuals' – anyone who wore glasses – even his inner circle could not ignore the madness. That he kept a pile of decapitated heads gathered from his enemies might have helped suppress overt expressions of dissatisfaction, but even fear can only last so long. When Macías had members of his own family killed, it signalled to his closest associates that no one was safe anymore. A coup was launched in 1979 and Macías attempted to flee with large amounts of cash but was swiftly captured. He had set fire to the rest of the country's cash supply before he left.

A trial was held and Macías found guilty of crimes against his country and people, which resulted in him being handed multiple death sentences. By the end of Macías' reign, tens of thousands had been killed by execution and starvation, and more than half of the country's population had fled.

BOKASSA I

Title inflation is a problem for most dictators. You might start as a general, but soon you have to be generalissimo, then president, then president for life … At some point, you either run out of titles or out of time. For Jean-Bédel Bokassa, the two ran out at around the same time.

Bokassa was born in 1921 in the French colony that is today the Central African Republic. When he was just six years old, his father, Mindogon Mgboundoulou, was murdered by the French authorities for an act they called rebellion. He freed a group of villagers held hostage by a French company, for which he was beaten to death in public. Bokassa's mother died soon afterwards.

Despite the rough treatment that shattered Bokassa's family, it was decided it would be best if he went to a French school if he was to have any hopes of advancement. At school, he took the name Jean-Bédel from that of an author of a book on French grammar. In 1939, Bokassa joined the French military and was soon pressed into service against the Axis powers when General de Gaulle called on colonial powers to reject Vichy control. Following World War II, he fought on the side of France in their colonial wars in Indochina.

When the French gave independence to the Central African Republic in 1960, Bokassa was superbly placed to profit from the new state of affairs. He was a cousin to David Dacko, the first president of the country and, with his time in the French military, was chosen to help train the fledgling nation's armed forces. Dacko soon transformed the country into one where only his political party was tolerated. Since he ran unopposed in 1964, Dacko was re-elected. But his government was plagued by inefficiency and waste, and the people of the Central African Republic were longing for change.

Dacko suspected that his cousin Bokassa was planning a military coup against him and tried raising a police force to oppose him, but it was too little, too late. In 1965, Bokassa struck first with his force of 500 soldiers by luring the head of the police to his army camp, arresting him and then occupying the capital. Dacko was forced to resign, though Bokassa gave him a familial hug beforehand. Bokassa named himself as the new president and tore up the constitution. He did at least tell the people there would be new elections, eventually.

Bokassa won popularity by claiming he was seeking out the people who had driven the country to poverty. Since he said that most civil servants did nothing other than sleep with their mistresses in their offices, they took the brunt of his ire. Bureaucrats who failed to support the new regime's aims of efficiency were arrested or forced into internal exile. Bokassa also set out to morally reform his nation. Though an enthusiastic lover of women, he banned other men from marrying multiple wives. He did put a stop to the genital mutilation of young girls, and crimes against women were treated with swift execution. Women seem to have liked these changes and would wipe the sweat from Bokassa's face with their dresses when he gave speeches. Bokassa was keen to win the support of Western powers and to be seen as a modernizer they could do business with.

Leaders do not rise on their own, and Bokassa's coup had been supported by another army commander called Alexandre Banza. When Banza wanted to curtail the new president's extravagance, Bokassa began to keep a loaded pistol close by in case anything happened when he and Banza would meet. Then, in 1969 Banza plotted a coup of his own. Bokassa crushed it quickly. Banza was captured, put in chains and dragged before Bokassa, who personally interrogated him by thrashing him with a walking stick. After a brief trial, Banza was shot by a firing squad and dumped in an unmarked grave, though other accounts have him savagely whipped, cut and beaten so badly his spine was obliterated before he was put out of his misery.

In 1972, Bokassa did away with the pretence that elections were always just around the corner by proclaiming himself president for life. Once officially in supreme power, his rule became more capricious and cruel: enemies were detained and placed in the harsh conditions of Ngaragba Prison, where they were beaten regularly. There were also rumours that Bokassa

IMPERIAL TRAPPINGS

Being an emperor comes with an upgrade to one's wardrobe. Bokassa ordered a ring with a black diamond shaped like Africa. The stone was almost worthless but he was told it was rare and invaluable. For the coronation itself, two crowns studded with huge – and genuinely valuable – diamonds were made at a cost of millions of dollars, nearly half of the annual budget of the entire country.

indulged in cannibalism. He is said to have quipped to a French diplomat after a banquet, 'You didn't notice, but you were eating human flesh.' Since there were plenty of diamonds in the Central African Republic, the French seemed willing to overlook a few crimes against humanity.

By 1976, Bokassa was not satisfied with simply being a general and president, and transformed his nation into the Central African Empire – with himself as Emperor Bokassa I. To maintain close relations, the French were encouraged to fund what would be one of the most lavish coronations ever.

The coronation was modelled on that of Napoleon and it was planned that the pope should crown Bokassa and his wife. Alas, the pope found other places to be, as did many of the heads of state Bokassa invited. The event took place in a basketball stadium where the air conditioning did not work. Many of the guests sweated uncomfortably through the interminable ceremony. At a feast afterwards, when the cake was cut, pigeons flew out. With parades, parties and thousands of bottles of wine, the coronation celebrations lasted two days – at a cost equal to one year of the empire's income.

While the emperor indulged in the wildest luxury, his subjects were starving. When they rioted in search of food, he ordered the military to fire on them. In 1979, Bokassa issued an edict ordering every student in the country to wear a special uniform with his image on it. Coincidentally, the uniforms were made by a company owned by his wife. When students protested this, about 100 were arrested. In the infamous Ngaragba Prison, Bokassa personally visited the students and beat a number to death with his walking stick before condemning the rest to similar demises.

When word of this atrocity got out, there was international outrage and the French instituted a coup to replace Bokassa with the former president Dacko. Bokassa was out of the country when the French forces arrived. They eventually offered Bokassa a place of safety in Paris, but he returned to the Central African Republic in 1986 and was placed on trial for his crimes. He was sentenced to death but this was commuted. He was released in 1993.

Towards the end of his life, Bokassa revealed he was the thirteenth apostle of Jesus. It would be the last title he would claim before he died in 1996.

ENVER HOXHA

. . . .

Tyrants try to leave their mark on their countries, but few have left as lasting a physical impact as Enver Hoxha did in Albania. Visitors to the country may notice a preponderance of small, grey concrete structures dotted almost everywhere and wonder what they are. These are the tens of thousands of bunkers which Hoxha ordered to be constructed to assuage his paranoia about invasion.

Hoxha was born in 1908 in Albania, though little is known about his childhood and youth. He studied at a school where French was spoken, and so was given a scholarship to study in France itself in 1930. There, he hinted that he was a communist, mainly to be invited to the riotous parties thrown by socialist socialites in Paris.

After this, he worked for some years in an Albanian consulate abroad, but no remarkable future seemed to lie ahead for the young man. After returning to Albania, he got a job as a teacher and might have ended up terrorizing children like any educator with a dictator complex. Then, during World War II when Albania was invaded and occupied by fascist Italy, Hoxha became seriously interested in politics, seeing communist ideology as an opposition to the fascist forces.

Hoxha was one of the leaders of the Communist Party of Albania from 1941. In 1942, he penned a 'Call to the Albanian Peasantry' in which he made the case for an uprising against the new puppet government. In it, he described how the Italians were like ravenous beasts feasting on the blood and sweat of Albanians. While the peasants of Albania were forced to harvest crops for the Axis forces, the invaders were harvesting anything of value from Albania. He told the people to resist in whatever way they could and to refuse to hand over anything the Italian-backed authorities demanded from them.

Nazi Germany succeeded Italy in occupying Albania in 1943, but the following year, the Axis forces in the country crumbled. Gradually, the Communist Party had become the dominant opposition force to the Nazis, and the Party named Hoxha as the interim prime minister. He set out for the capital in a confiscated car, partisans who had been fighting for Albanian freedom flanking the convoy holding the new government. The crowds who saw the 36-year-old man emerge for a liberation parade would have had a hard time recognizing Hoxha, who was not then a well-known figure. But with a raised fist he announced he was in charge, though they did not know then that he would never give up power. Despite promises of leading a democratic nation, from its earliest days, the Hoxha regime was nakedly communist.

Reprisals against those who had collaborated with the fascists were swift. As soon as the capital, Tirana, fell into his hands, Hoxha sent an order that all traitors were to be arrested. His followers visited the homes of those on the list and dragged them to the basement of a hotel. Without even the rudiments of a trial, they were shot on the spot. Most never knew why they had been taken.

Hoxha was heavily influenced by the policies of Josef Stalin, and his own account of a meeting between the two in 1949 reveals his admiration for Stalin – while also noting the dangers of working with him. When Hoxha was invited to speak with Stalin, he greeted the Soviet leader by announcing, 'May you live another hundred years, Comrade Stalin!' Stalin narrowed his eyes and commented that a mere hundred years did not seem like nearly long enough. Curiously, Stalin in Hoxha's versions of these meetings comes across as the more reasonable of the two. When Hoxha suggested Albanians would rather die than give up any territory, it was Stalin who suggested diplomacy might be preferable to death.

Intellectuals are always a risk for tyrants – they tend to be able to think of better alternatives than life under a dictator,

FIGHTING BACK

One of those arrested in this round up of so-called dissidents was the prosperous businessman Jonuz Kaceli. According to some accounts, while he was being interrogated Kaceli managed to punch Mehmet Shehu, Hoxha's thuggish henchman, in the face. For this crime, Kaceli was unceremoniously thrown out of a window to his death.

and so they are often marked for liquidation. In 1951, a small bomb detonated at the Soviet embassy in Tirana. Twenty-three people who had already been selected as an intellectual threat to the state were arrested on Hoxha's orders and accused of treason for the attack. All were executed. Among those marked for death was a former classmate of Hoxha, Sabiha Kasimati, one of the first female scientists in Albania. She had made the mistake of once mocking Hoxha at school.

The Sigurimi, the secret police, were active at this time, hunting out any deviation from communist orthodoxy. Their investigations doomed thousands to either execution or gulags where many were worked to death. Albanian emigrants who had fled abroad were closely monitored so they could be targeted for elimination. Twenty million documents gathered by thousands of secret police informers still survive. Escaping the country was difficult – three boys who dreamed of fleeing to Greece, where people had such luxuries as televisions and cars, were arrested, and two of them killed, after their teacher informed the Sigurimi.

Following the death of Stalin in 1953, Albania found itself increasingly isolated from the Soviet Union on which it depended for economic support. Hoxha was forced to turn to the Chinese communists for aid. He had ambitious plans for modernizing Albania's industry but he needed money and labour to do it. After Mao launched his Cultural Revolution in China, in 1967 Hoxha decided he needed one of his own. Writers and artists who might be disloyal or subversive in their work were purged. The army's loyalty was assured by placing political monitors among the troops. Religion, Marx's opium of the masses, was crushed, and Albania declared itself to be the world's first atheist state.

With Soviet and Western threats so close, Hoxha instituted a policy of building bunkers to fortify every inch of Albania. These bunkers were mostly small shelters just large enough for two soldiers, from which they could fire at invaders. Creating over 100,000 of these bunkers drained the resources of an already overstretched nation. Poverty in Albania was not helped by the banning of foreign investment: Hoxha decreed that his nation should be self-reliant. By the time he died, Albania was one of the poorest nations on Earth.

Hoxha survived until 1985. His paranoia was undimmed until almost the very end. Mehmet Shehu, who had supported Hoxha for nearly forty years and acted as his strongman in battling dissidents, was accused of treason in 1981. Despite all his work for Hoxha, it was announced that Shehu had 'committed suicide'.

HASTINGS BANDA

One of the side effects of being a dictator is that you might find yourself becoming inexplicably wealthy. Somehow money seems to end up in the hands of tyrants. It is almost as if those with absolute power treat the money supplies of their countries as an extension of their own personal bank accounts. When this happens, such a regime is termed a kleptocracy – and Hastings Banda of Malawi was one of the most accomplished kleptocrats of the twentieth century.

Banda's early life is something of a mystery. For instance, his date of birth has been placed at anywhere between 1886 and 1906, as birth certificates were not issued at the time in what was then the British Protectorate of Nyasaland. The year 1898 seems the most likely for his birth. He was named Akim Kamnkhwala Mtunthama Banda, but when he was later baptized into the Church of Scotland, he took the name Hastings Banda in honour of a missionary he liked.

Banda travelled in southern Africa by walking to various educational facilities and to South Africa for work. His interest in medicine was prompted by witnessing the poor health care that was available to Africans. He genuinely seems to have wanted to help people, and pursuing a medical career would expose Banda to the wider world.

In 1925, and with the help of a Christian charity, Banda went to the USA to study, earning multiple degrees with additional financial support from various philanthropists. In 1937, he was only the second person from Malawi to gain a medical degree. But if Banda wished to practise medicine in the British Empire, he would have to get a medical degree from a British university, and so he travelled to Edinburgh in 1938.

MODEL DICTATOR

Banda was always immaculately dressed whenever he appeared in public. He was renowned for his perfectly cut three-piece suits which he would wear with a crisp tie and colour-matched handkerchief in his pocket. His head was often adorned with the Homburg hat that was fashionable in the Edwardian era. To set off the outfit, he carried a fly whisk in his hand. Banda had strong opinions on how others dressed and once fled a room where a man dared to sit without wearing shoes or socks. When in power, he banned women from wearing trousers.

While there, Banda continued to receive stipends from a couple of groups, neither of which was aware of the other's financial aid, which allowed him to live well. He also met several people who would be influential in African colonies winning their independence – a topic about which Banda was becoming more vocal. Though Banda was proudly a member of the Church of Scotland, and dressed in the finest English fashions, he did not want his people eternally under the thumb of the British.

Dr Banda was by all accounts a skilled medical man and loved by his patients when he practised in Britain. He was known to refuse payment from poor people seeking help. Banda used some of the money he earned at this time to sponsor the education of other Africans. How then did this doctor transform into a dictator?

Banda suffered a number of personal setbacks. He had formed a relationship with the married Merene French, and when her husband filed for divorce, Banda was named in the court documents – a shameful event for a professional man. Banda ended his relationship with Merene when he moved to Ghana in 1951. Another disturbing issue was Britain's plan to federate Nyasaland with Rhodesia, a scheme which Banda thought was designed simply to maintain white supremacy.

Banda gained a reputation in his homeland as a well-educated, intelligent and kindly man who believed in self-rule. The independence movement felt that he would be a unifying figure for a young nation as well as a politician familiar with British leaders. Banda was already an older man with a career outside of politics, so the activists thought that he would appeal as a temporary leader who would soon step down once he was put in power. These hopes were to be dashed.

In 1958, Banda returned to Nyasaland and was welcomed as the new head of the self-rule movement. Within years, the country was granted independence from Britain, and in 1964, the nation of Malawi (the name chosen by Banda) was born. Banda was elected as the first prime minister, but members of the cabinet already feared he was leaning towards dictatorship. When they proposed limiting his powers, he sacked several ministers and others resigned, fleeing the country. An attempted rebellion was put down. In 1966, Banda turned the country into a republic and became its first president in an election with no other candidates. This position was soon made lifelong, with no further need for elections. Banda framed his rule by decree, as was traditional for chiefs in Nyasaland, but he would not allow the lengthy debates which chiefs had normally taken part in.

Banda was treated as the sole saviour of his nation. Everything that could be named in his honour was, from roads to airports. To ensure that the nation kept up with his political beliefs, he formed the Malawi Young Pioneers, a group of youths who were originally trained to aid citizens in rural development. However, they soon became enforcers and informers for Banda. To help manage his people, television was banned and only one newspaper was printed.

Despite his kindly appearance, Banda presided over one of Africa's most repressive and autocratic regimes, imposing a culture of fear, murdering thousands of suspected dissidents or those who did not conform to his strict social ideas, and detaining many more without trial. In 1983, Banda's rule was challenged by three ministers. He had them seized, and then stripped the parliament of the last shreds of its authority. The ministers were tortured, and when another member of parliament just happened to wander by and witness the atrocity, he too was seized. The four were killed by having tent pegs beaten into their skulls. To hide the murders, the bodies were placed in a car and an accident was staged.

Banda had been a powerful voice against communism in Africa and so his eccentric rule was tolerated and supported by Western powers. With the fall of the Soviet Union, however, he was no longer a useful ally. Internal unrest and external pressure pushed Banda to allow free elections in 1994, which he lost. He was put on trial for several of the murders his regime had committed, but was found innocent. He retired to enjoy the fruits of his despotism. It is thought that over his lifetime he siphoned off several hundred million dollars from Malawi's economy. Even though he died in 1997, it is still a mystery where all this money ended up.

FERDINAND MARCOS

Ferdinand Marcos, dictator of the Philippines, is said to have been introduced to the brutal realities of politics from a young age. His father, Mariano Marcos, was a lawyer and politician who suffered several humiliating election defeats to Julio Nalundasan. In 1935, Nalundasan was found dead in his home with a single rifle shot to the head. Suspicion immediately fell on the Marcos family and four of them, including Mariano and eighteen-year-old Ferdinand, were put on trial for the murder in 1938. Mariano was found innocent but Ferdinand was found guilty and given a long sentence in prison. This was mainly because Ferdinand was on his university's rifle team, with which he had won several shooting competitions, and because the weapon used in the attack was one he had access to. On appeal, Ferdinand's conviction was quashed by a judge who saw it as merely a youthful indiscretion. Ferdinand completed his legal studies and graduated at the top of his class in 1939.

Having been in the Reserve Officer Training Corps, Marcos was called up for service when the Japanese attacked the Philippines in 1941. He fought with the United States army for a time and would later claim to have earned a staggering number of medals – twenty-seven including the Medal of Honour – which would have made him one of the most decorated soldiers in Philippine history. However, no evidence of these awards being bestowed, or the heroics behind them, has yet been uncovered.

It is known that he was captured by the Japanese in 1942 but he was released under uncertain circumstances. It seems that Marcos was set free as his father was collaborating with Japanese forces. Towards the end of the war, Mariano was attacked by guerrilla freedom fighters and executed by being tied to cattle and torn apart. His body parts were displayed as a warning to others.

When Ferdinand Marcos emerged from the war, he claimed to have been one of the chief leaders of the guerrillas who had opposed the Japanese. He asked for millions of dollars from the Americans as compensation for material support he had given – oddly, no evidence of these services was found, either.

With a seemingly glittering war record to boast of, in 1949 Marcos succeeded in gaining election to the House of Representatives in the independent Philippines which had emerged in 1946. After two decades of ever greater positions in parliament, he ran for the presidency in 1965 and, accompanied on the campaign by his glamorous wife Imelda, he won by offering popular policies. There were also accusations of vote-buying.

EDIFICE COMPLEX

Most dictators are builders who love to erect grand edifices to celebrate their glories. In the Philippines, Ferdinand and Imelda Marcos used some of the funds raised through foreign loans to construct so many monumental buildings that it was claimed they had an 'Edifice Complex'. Among other structures, they built modern bridges, luxury hotels and a large 'Coconut Palace' to house guests. Much of the work was done at great speed. While building the Manila Film Center, a scaffolding collapse killed 169 labourers by plunging them into wet cement.

Marcos' first term in office had given him a great deal of popularity, but at the 1969 elections he refused to rely on the fondness of his people. His campaign spent nearly a hundred times as much money as his opponent. In case that failed, he also used the police and gangs to intimidate those who might vote against him. Unsurprisingly, Marcos triumphed. The public spending splurge he engaged in left the Philippines teetering on the brink of economic collapse.

The failing economy sparked many to question whether Marcos was the right person to lead the country. On one occasion, after he gave a speech to parliament, demonstrators chased him and his wife until they were whisked away to safety. In 1971, there was a bombing at a campaign rally for an opposition party which killed nine and injured nearly a hundred. Marcos was quick to blame communist agitators, and when other bombings followed, he used them as a pretext to suspend the normal rule of law. Evidence has since emerged that these bombings may have been planned by Marcos himself.

From 1972, Marcos ruled under martial law. This move to give him almost total control was ratified by a referendum in which more than 90 per cent of people apparently approved it. Just before Marcos made his declaration, there was a crackdown on the freedom of the press, which somewhat muted the public response to the announcement. Once martial law was in effect, Marcos was free to arrest anyone who seemed to be a threat to him. Students and others who had led the demonstrations against him were rounded up. Torture, both physical and sexual, was employed against prisoners. During Marcos' rule, many opponents turned up dead under unexplained circumstances.

Under the dictatorship of Ferdinand Marcos, his family and friends profited handsomely, being rewarded with plum government jobs and positions in industry. This gave Marcos control over almost the entire state and allowed his cronies to steal millions of dollars. For instance, a Coconut Levy Fund – a tax on coconut farmers that was meant to be put back into the development of the coconut industry – raised hundreds of millions of dollars that somehow disappeared into private hands.

It is unknown just how much money the Marcos family gained during their rule of the Philippines. Assessments are all in the billions of dollars. Imelda Marcos' collection of more than 3,000 pairs of shoes is just the most famous example of their kleptocratic wealth. Imelda also held a vast collection of artworks, and her jewellery included huge diamonds, rubies and emeralds, the value of which could each have fed thousands of people for years. Half of the Philippines was living in poverty at the time.

Marcos repealed martial law in 1981 but retained his control of the state. In an election that year, he managed to win again in a suspiciously large landslide. When Ninoy Aquino, a key leader of the opposition, returned from self-imposed exile to the Philippines in 1983, he was shot dead as he left his aircraft. But the people were tiring of years of corruption under the Marcos family and, in 1986, popular demonstrations rose up against the regime. Marcos called an election and Aquino's widow, Corazon, ran to topple him. Corazon Aquino seems to have won, but official results gave the victory to Marcos.

The People Power Revolution of that year saw Marcos ousted when his military allies abandoned him. He was forced to flee and spent the rest of his life in exile in Hawaii, dying in 1989. His exile was softened by the large amount of loot he took with him.

In 2022, Marcos' son, Ferdinand 'Bongbong' Marcos, was elected as the president of the Philippines. Memories of dictatorship can apparently be short.

KIM JONG IL

There is perhaps no tyranny more successful, at least for the tyrants, than North Korea. Their leadership is unquestioned. The whole world has seen videos of North Korean dictators strolling in front of adoring crowds who burst into tears with the joy of being in their presence. Applause for their least statement is long and enthusiastic. Whenever the despots inspect a new factory or school, they are attended by a gaggle of military men whose uniforms are covered in ranks of gaudy medals – each holding a notebook to jot down the least word of wisdom their leader lets slip.

That is the public face of the regime. However, those who defect from North Korea speak of a land of grinding misery. People support the regime because if they do not there will be the most brutal consequences for both them and their families. Work camps – concentration camps in all but name – dot the landscape for those who transgress against the state. Executions are common and painful. It is said that high-ranking members of the party leadership who disappoint their master have been torn apart by dogs.

Kim Jong Il was the supreme leader of North Korea from 1994 until his death in 2011, though he technically remains its Eternal Leader. As we have seen, many dictators try to pass on their power only for their heir to prove a disappointment and fall. Instead, in many regards the modern history of North Korea is the history of the Kim family that has ruled it since the end of World War II.

The dynasty was founded by Kim Il Sung, father of Kim Jong Il. Given the extreme nature of North Korean propaganda, it can be difficult to discern the truth about Il Sung's early life. According to their sources, he trained at a military academy and helped to found an early communist movement. After moving to China, he fought against the Japanese invaders of Manchuria. When the Chinese communists suspected Koreans of supporting the Japanese, Kim was investigated but cleared, though thousands of other Koreans were purged. Kim burned the archives of the committee leading the purge, making many Korean fighters turn to him as a leader.

When the Soviets occupied North Korea in 1945, they appointed Kim Il Sung as their preferred leader. It was he who created an army of party loyalists and set about turning the country into a communist paradise. Backed with Soviet arms, the North Koreans invaded the south with the aim of claiming all the Korean peninsula. The Korean War which followed turned into a proxy war between the Western democracies and the communist powers. By the time the war ended in 1953,

Kim Il Sung was undisputed master of the north. He preached a doctrine of self-reliance, meaning that North Korea cut itself off from much of the world in terms of trade and diplomacy. The people were put to work in heavy industry. According to North Korean propaganda, whenever Kim Il Sung visited one of his factories the workers were so touched by his divine presence their output tripled. This was just the beginning of the cult of personality surrounding the North Korean leaders.

Kim Jong Il, heir to Kim Il Sung, was born under a shining star – literally. According to North Korean legend, when Kim Jong Il entered the world on 16 February 1941 or 1942, a bright star appeared in the sky to herald his birth. The day is still celebrated each year in North Korea. As son of the supreme leader, Kim Jong Il was guaranteed success in the regime. He got his start by running the propaganda department of the government, where he quickly learned how to maintain an aura of authority.

By 1980, although his father was still in command and worshipped as the founder of the state, Kim Jong Il was being referred to as the 'Dear Leader'. In many regards, he was in control from this point forwards, and assumed the leadership of the army. The Korean People's Army is one of the largest in the world and most civilians receive training with weapons. He was also suspected of ordering acts of terrorism and bombings in South Korea.

When Kim Il Sung died in 1994, it was immediately announced that Kim Jong Il was officially taking over. His father's funeral took place against the backdrop of wailing crowds lining every road in the capital. Kim Jong Il celebrated the legacy of his father and by doing so celebrated himself. According to defectors, every single publication, television programme and film serves the purpose of proclaiming the glories of the Kim family.

A MAN OF MANY TALENTS

According to North Korean sources, there was almost nothing that Kim Jong Il could not do. The first time he played a round of golf it is said that he scored eleven holes-in-one. His fashion sense was so good that it was announced the whole world was taking up his style. He was also credited with inventing a new dish that seems suspiciously similar to a hamburger. Among his many talents which were trumpeted by the state was the fact that Kim Jong Il had no need to go to the toilet.

Behind the glossy image portrayed by the North Koreans, the dark horrors of life for the people grew grimmer. Isolation may have given the Kims a greater control of their nation, but it also stagnated the economy and pushed the people into poverty. Starvation was common and sporadic reports of cannibalism emerged. To hide the true nature of life in North Korea, foreigners are only allowed in certain places where their experience is closely controlled and they are shown only model hotels and supermarkets which are kept stocked merely to impress visitors.

The higher members of the party are said to live in some style, even as they exist in fear of making a mistake which may lead to them being purged. The common people simply live in fear. No one lived better than Kim Jong Il. He imported the finest foods and drinks from abroad at great expense even as his people struggled to feed themselves. The famine of the late 1990s killed hundreds of thousands, and perhaps millions.

In 2011, Kim Jong Il died. It was said that a marvellous light glowed over the mountain where he was born. Power was transferred to his son Kim Jong Un, who has continued the strict dictatorship of his ancestors. To ensure that no one could threaten his rule, Kim Jong Un had his brother Kim Jong-nam assassinated by poison in Malaysia. Since the Kims control a vast army and nuclear weaponry, the rest of the world seems unwilling to risk provoking them. The North Koreans will have to live, if they can, under the Kims for some time to come.

SADDAM HUSSEIN

Few dictators get the chance to lose two wars to the United States of America. The usual etiquette is to be killed or commit suicide after the Americans defeat you. Saddam Hussein of Iraq holds the rare distinction of being defeated spectacularly twice by a coalition headed by the USA.

Saddam's early life was not ideal. His father had died before Saddam's birth in 1937 and his mother attempted to abort him. On his mother's remarriage, his stepfather was brutal towards

the young boy and Saddam fled to live with relatives. After dropping out of university, he joined the Ba'ath Party, which worked for freedom for Arab nations and a form of socialism, though one deeply opposed to communism.

One of Saddam's first political acts for the Ba'athists was to take part in the attempted assassination of the prime minister of Iraq, Abdul-Karim Qasim, in 1959. As Qasim's convoy drove through Baghdad, a group of Ba'athist assassins aimed to shoot him and his associates. According to some sources, Saddam opened fire too early and the assassination attempt descended into chaos. Qasim survived with minor injuries and Saddam was forced to flee abroad. However, the legend of Saddam's daring action functioned to raise his profile and win him support among disaffected Iraqis.

Qasim was overthrown and executed in 1963 and the Ba'athist party rose to power – but briefly. In turn, the Ba'athists were driven out and purged. However, in the short window of Ba'athist government, Saddam returned to Iraq. He was imprisoned for some time but continued to rise in the ranks of the party. When the Ba'athists came to power again in 1968, Saddam, then in charge of the security service, was named as the vice president. He became hugely popular at this time because a boom in oil profits allowed him to spend lavishly on improving the state. Saddam was canny enough to coerce or bribe journalists to sing his praises. When he was made head of Iraq's armed forces, the true control of the nation lay in his hands.

When the president of Iraq, Ahmad Hasan al-Bakr, attempted to unify his nation with Syria, this proved a threat to Saddam's ascendency and he acted quickly. In 1979, Saddam forced the president to resign and took his place. Within days, he set about purging the Ba'athist party of anyone with even a hint of disloyalty. At a recorded meeting of the party's leadership, Saddam sat quietly puffing on a cigar while a list of traitors was read out and sixty-eight accused were led from the room. Many of those taken away were executed.

Some of the changes that Saddam brought about were positive, such as equality for women, who were encouraged to attend university and enter the professions. But these improvements were backed by harsh repression in all areas of civil rights. Freedom of movement and expression were heavily curtailed and only members of the Ba'ath Party were considered to be full citizens.

Saddam was fearful of both internal and external threats to his rule. When Iran underwent an Islamic revolution in 1979, he worried that it would spill over into his country. Tensions flared along the border and both sides tried to undermine the other. In 1980, with Iraqi support, a group of rebel Iranians captured the Iranian embassy in London and held those inside hostage. That year, Iraq invaded Iran, beginning a bloody and costly war that proved to be a stalemate. Over the next eight years, hundreds of thousands of soldiers died on both sides and billions of dollars were wasted. Fighting laid waste to the oil fields of Iraq and left the country facing ruin.

It was during and after this war that Saddam launched a campaign of genocide against the Kurdish people living in the north of Iraq, whom he considered a threat to his security. Troops, aircraft and tanks were sent in to attack villages, and Saddam also turned chemical weapons on the Kurds. Around 100,000 Kurds died in this campaign.

With the economic devastation of the Iran–Iraq war, Saddam needed money, but oil prices were too low to allow him to earn enough. He turned on Kuwait – which was far wealthier than Iraq – accusing Kuwaitis of drilling into Iraqi oil reservoirs, and in 1990, launched an invasion. Unfortunately for Saddam, the Western powers were heavily invested in Kuwait and needed their cheap oil. A US-led coalition was launched to liberate Kuwait and, in just a few weeks, the Iraqi army was humiliatingly pushed out. Tens of thousands of Iraqis died and more were taken captive.

Saddam Hussein was able to cling to power thanks to his government's machinery of terror. People were taken into prison and abused along with their loved ones, sometimes tortured in front of each other. Executions were often public as a warning to others. Members of the Ba'ath party were legally immune from prosecution for whatever they did, so long as it was performed to protect the regime.

This immunity from any consequences led people to act on their basest impulses with impunity. Saddam's son, Uday, was famed for his cruelty and impulsive actions. He was fond of

WRITTEN IN BLOOD

Saddam does not seem to have been notably pious in his religion, but played on his faith to bolster support against the West. In 1997, he commissioned an extraordinary copy of the Quran. This book, he said, was written in his own blood and he claimed to have donated sixty pints of blood to its production. Writing the Quran in blood was widely condemned by many Muslims as blasphemy. Doubts also emerged that Saddam had given any blood to the endeavour – likely much of it came from unwilling 'volunteers'.

firing guns during random, drunken parties, and taking drugs, which did not aid his mental stability. Uday was personally responsible for rapes, murders and tortures. As the head of the Iraqi Football Association, he once had the national team beaten on the soles of their feet after a defeat. No shame he brought on the regime seemed to harm his position.

The USA continued to view Iraq with suspicion, fearing that Iraq was developing weapons of mass destruction and was supporting terrorist groups. Saddam had presented himself as a rival to the West and now the West called his bluff. In 2003, a US-led coalition invaded Iraq to remove the potential threat by ousting Saddam. Iraqi resistance crumbled in the face of overwhelming attacks, and Saddam's sons and grandson were shot down.

Saddam fled from Baghdad and his whereabouts remained a mystery for several months. When he was finally captured, he was discovered in a small pit hidden under a rug. He was put on trial for his crimes against the Iraqi people and was hanged in 2006 as a crowd shouted, 'Go to hell' at him.

MUAMMAR GADDAFI

Tyrants may wish that their dictatorships would never end, but the best they can realistically hope for is that they will die peacefully in bed. But when a tyrant falls, they often fall hard. Fewer have had a harder landing than Muammar Gaddafi of Libya.

Gaddafi was born into a Bedouin tribe and no records were kept of his birth, but it was likely in 1942. His family, who were goatherds, managed to scrape together the funds needed to see that he received an education in a nearby town. It was during this time that Gaddafi started mixing with people who believed in freeing Arabs from Western influence. In the wake of World War II, Libya had been made into a monarchy which was favourable to the Americans and Europeans. Gaddafi was expelled from his school for taking part in demonstrations against this.

Coming from poverty and without family connections, Gaddafi joined the Libyan army to make his way in the world. He struggled during training as he viewed the British agents in charge of the education of soldiers as agents of imperialism. As soon as his training was complete, Gaddafi organized a secret group of fellow officers whose aim was revolution, but who expected that they would have to bide their time. In fact, they did not have to wait long.

The Libyan monarchy was increasingly unpopular with its subjects and several plots were forming against King Idris. In 1969, while the king was out of the country, Gaddafi and his supporters launched their coup. Almost as soon as it was announced, army units flocked to support the rebellion and all the important infrastructure of Libya was taken into their hands. Gaddafi declared a new Libyan republic to be led by himself and his colleagues. Eschewing grandiose titles, Gaddafi was content to be known simply as Colonel Gaddafi.

Gaddafi was in a good position to negotiate with the Western powers since Libya had recently discovered large amounts of oil in its territory. By threatening to cut off access to this oil, Gaddafi was able to get favourable terms on almost everything he desired. Within Libya, he set about reforming the state to sweep away the decadence and inequalities of the monarchy. With oil money flowing in, Libya prospered and Gaddafi's regime did too. Many people in Libya experienced an increased standard of living at this time. Reflecting his origins in the countryside, Gaddafi instituted the building of new villages with modern amenities and relocated people to them.

Repression soon followed, however. In 1973, Gaddafi issued a decree that all opponents to his revolution had to be removed. The state soon began to look into the political purity of the people and control their way of life. In 1976, students at Libyan universities demonstrated against the regime and called for greater democracy. Supporters of Gaddafi fought back and many of the students were taken away and imprisoned. Held in jail for a year, they were brought out to be publicly executed on the anniversary of their rallies. For years afterwards on the same day, enemies of the state were killed to commemorate Gaddafi's crushing of the students. Sometimes executions took place in stadiums packed with children bussed in to watch the spectacle as part of their education. To ensure greater compliance with the regime's aims, committees were set up to monitor the activities of the people.

Libya's oil money gave Gaddafi influence beyond its borders, and Libyan oil made many nations want to keep Libya on their side. He was able to buy support from other African leaders. While Libya declared itself to be a socialist country in 1977 and had good relations with the Soviet Union, it maintained its independence.

Those Libyans who fled abroad to avoid being caught by Gaddafi's zealous followers found that no distance from home was truly safe. Libyan exiles had the unusual tendency of ending up with a bullet hole in their head. International borders meant little to Gaddafi's agents and Libya was a key sponsor of terrorist groups throughout his rule. His most deadly attack came in 1988 when a bomb exploded aboard a Pan Am flight over the town of Lockerbie in Scotland, killing 270 people.

Gaddafi became increasingly eccentric over the years, even as he remained dangerous to both friends and foes. One of his desires was to always be surrounded by beautiful women. A group of female guards known as the Revolutionary Nuns was responsible for Gaddafi's safety. They always appeared immaculately made-up and armed with guns. It was details like this that obsessed many while they ignored the darker aspects of his rule. These ladies were sworn to celibacy, but Gaddafi took no such vow – beneath his palaces were chambers where unspeakable acts of non-consensual sexual depravity occurred.

BACK TO THE BEDOUIN

Gaddafi liked to play up his Bedouin origin by dressing in traditional clothes, drinking copious amounts of camel milk and sleeping as often as possible in a tent. When foreign dignitaries arrived in Libya, Gaddafi often greeted them in a tent. When he travelled abroad, he frequently took a special bulletproof tent to sleep in.

The Gaddafi regime could not survive forever. Torture and disappearances were common, and people who ended up in prison were faced with horrifically poor conditions. When those held in Abu Salim Prison on trumped-up charges protested against their treatment, more than 1,000 of them were killed. Some were placed on buses and taken to an unknown fate while the rest were executed by shooting on the spot.

In 2011, the Arab world was shaken by a series of uprisings by populations fed up with corruption and repressive regimes. In February of that year, Libyans took to the streets against Gaddafi. He unleashed troops on his own people and murdered hundreds. Rape was used against women by his men as a form of terror.

The Western powers offered aid to the rebels and members of the ruling party started to defect to the rebels when they saw how events were likely to turn out. Gaddafi was forced from the capital. He was cornered by rebel forces and captured after being injured by a grenade which had been poorly thrown by his own men. Gaddafi was hiding in a drain when he was dragged out to suffer the most humiliating execution. Videos were recorded showing the bloodied dictator being forced to stumble in front of a baying crowd. Some show unspeakable things being done to Gaddafi before he was shot dead.

SAPARMURAT NIYAZOV

. . . .

Turkmenistan in Central Asia became one of the republics of the Soviet Union in 1924, and its 5 million inhabitants toiled in a mostly agrarian society supplying goods to the USSR. It was in 1940 that Saparmurat Atayevich Niyazov was born in a village near the capital. He would not remain simply Saparmurat Niyazov however – in time he came to be known as the Eternal Sun of Turkmenistan, All-powerful and Fearless Serdar (Leader), and Turkmenbashi (Lord of All Turkmen) the Great.

Niyazov's rise to power was typical of those who flourished under the Soviet system. As a loyal communist, he was given ever greater positions of authority and might have been just another functionary in their governmental machine had the reform-minded Mikhail Gorbachev not become leader of the USSR in 1985. Among Gorbachev's first acts was the removal on the grounds of corruption of Muhammetnazar Gapurow as the First Secretary of the Central Committee of the Communist Party of Turkmenistan, replacing him with Niyazov.

By the late 1980s, the Soviet Union was beginning to fall apart under economic and social pressures. Nationalism in the various Soviet republics was on the rise and added a further force tugging the USSR towards disintegration. What was needed to distract the people from thinking about national identity was a strong man who would become the focus of everyone's attention. Niyazov filled the role and started to construct a cult of personality.

The legislature of Turkmenistan declared independence after the fall of the USSR and an election was held to decide who would become president of the new nation. Only one person was on the ballot, Niyazov himself. With nearly every citizen apparently voting, Niyazov was declared the victor with more than 99 per cent of votes cast for him.

Niyazov knew that decades of Soviet leadership had left his country unprepared for entry into the modern world economy. So he set Turkmenistan on a path of modernization, creating the infrastructure to reap the benefits of textiles, cotton and, most importantly, oil and gas. Luckily for Turkmenistan, it sits atop some of the largest reserves of oil and gas in the world – where there are fossil fuels, there will soon be foreign investors.

The bizarre projects enacted by this autocrat caught the attention of the world's media and made the absolute ruler of Turkmenistan famous in a way few other leaders of former Soviet states were. The trade in fossil fuels has supported many a dictator, but few have used it to fund quite so many strange monuments.

In the capital city of Ashgabat, you could find the Monument of Neutrality, erected to celebrate Turkmenistan maintaining peace with its neighbours. Atop the 75-metre tripod was a 12-metre-tall statue of Niyazov, plated in pure gold, to look down over his city and all the benefits his rule had brought. Of course, you would not want any shadows to mar the beauty of this sculpture, so it was placed on a rotating base that turned to ensure Niyazov always faced the sun. Those who wanted to see their leader more closely need only look at the nearest wall where posters and portraits would likely be hanging.

The whim of a tyrant is the word of the law. Following a heart attack, and belatedly learning the dangers of smoking, Niyazov banned his cabinet from smoking and prohibited smoking in public places. He appointed the education ministry to check that young men were not growing their hair long or growing beards. Gold teeth were banned because, Niyazov insisted, teeth could be strengthened naturally by chewing on soup bones. Drivers could not listen to radios in their cars. Opera is not to everyone's taste, and the dictator banned performances as they were deemed superfluous to state requirements. Libraries outside of the capital city were closed, but they were also unnecessary because Niyazov had written the only book worth reading.

MELONS

After deciding that a melon named after him tasted like the fruit of paradise, Niyazov ordered an annual public holiday in its honour. Melon Day is still celebrated on the second Sunday in August each year.

In 1990, it was revealed that a vision had come to Niyazov which showed him how to make his country great. The thoughts prompted by this revelation were turned into a book called the *Ruhnama* ('Book of the Soul') which contains everything from political musings to poetry and historical accounts of dubious accuracy. The book became something of a proxy for the man himself. It was set up in places of religious devotion, displayed ostentatiously on desks, and study of it became mandatory. If you wished to have a driving licence, finish school or work in the government, then you had to pass a test on the *Ruhnama*. If you found the book too heavy to lift, then you could tune into one of the television programmes which regularly broadcast sections of it.

So much for the maniac, what about the monster? While some in the West might have been amused by the vulgar eccentricities of the great Turkmenbashi, the realities of life under his rule were less funny. For all the wealth created by trade in natural gas, most people remained relatively poor, while Niyazov somehow personally amassed billions of dollars.

Perhaps fortunately, no one lives forever. Niyazov died suddenly in 2006 and, after a great outpouring of mourning, was buried in a grand mausoleum he had already constructed. But without the man there to reinforce the rule, his successor slowly began dismantling some of the cult of personality. The golden statue of Niyazov was removed from the centre of the capital and people were allowed to call the days of the week by their old names. Even the study of Niyazov's immortal book was relaxed.

AFTERWORD

In 1989, the historian Francis Fukuyama published a paper with the title 'The End of History?' This was not a doom-laden work about the imminent demise of the world but rather one in which he announced that the liberal democracies had essentially 'won' history. They would triumph and other systems of government were doomed to failure. History would end because everyone seemed to agree that we had come up with the best form of politics.

The years since then have not been very kind to this thesis. For a while, it seemed to be right. The Soviet Union fell and was replaced with a democracy which was open to diplomacy and trade with the West. But as all the world knows, since then Russia has fallen into a bellicose kleptocracy under one-man rule where dissenters to the regime have the troubling habit of falling out of windows.

Other countries around the world have seen despots dethroned, only for new ones to take their place a few years later. Or, even in so-called 'free' democracies, human rights and civil liberties have sometimes come under threat. Democracy is only secure against tyrants as long as the majority vote against would-be authoritarians – if they are elected, there is little that can be done afterwards to oust them.

So, as we have seen in this book, there is no end to history. It seems that there will be always be those who want to seize the reins of the state for their own benefit. They may dress up their ambition as being for the good of the majority, but somehow they always end up the ones living in a palace while their people suffer.

Tyrants, or the personality types who desire to be a tyrant, will always be with us, partly because I believe there is an itch of greed inside us all. Most of us only scratch it by having one more biscuit than we need, but for some the desire for wealth and power has no limit. The rest of us consider that freedom and democracy are worth fighting for. The only problem is that the fight never ends.

SELECT BIBLIOGRAPHY

Abbott, Elizabeth. *Haiti: A Shattered Nation*. Overlook Press, 2011.

Fevziu, Blendi. *Enver Hoxha: The Iron Fist of Albania*. Bloomsbury Academic, 2022.

Herodotus. *The Histories*. Translated by Aubrey de Sélincourt. Penguin, 2003.

Hochschild, Adam. *King Leopold's Ghost: A Story of Greed, Terror and Heroism in Colonial Africa*. Pan Books, 2012.

Kenyon, Paul. *Dictatorland: The Men Who Stole Africa*. Head of Zeus, 2018.

Plutarch. *Parallel Lives*. Various translations.

Rees, Laurence. *Hitler and Stalin: The Tyrants and World War II*. Viking, 2020.

Roberts, Andrew. *Napoleon the Great*. Penguin, 2015.

Schama, Simon. *Citizens: Chronicle of the French Revolution*. Penguin, 2004.

Titley, Brian. *Dark Age: The Political Odyssey of Emperor Bokassa*. McGill-Queen's University Press, 2002.

INDEX